JOSEPH CONRAD: A STUDY IN NON-CONFORMITY

JOSEPH CONRAD

A Study in Non-conformity

Osborn Andreas

ARCHON BOOKS
1969

SBN: 208 00790 3
Library of Congress Catalog Card Number: 69-19211
Printed in the United States of America

TABLE OF CONTENTS

CHAPTER

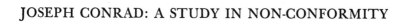

JOSEPH CONRAD: A STUDY IN NON-CONFORMITY

Chapter 1.

THE BLACK MATE

JOSEPH CONRAD's last literary act was to publish the first story he ever wrote: THE BLACK MATE, written in 1884 and suppressed (except for magazine publication) until 1924. The writing of THE BLACK MATE took place eleven years before his first published work, ALMAYER'S FOLLY, appeared in print. Why did Conrad permit twenty-four years to elapse between the writing and the magazine publication of this story, and then exclude it from his collected short stories for another sixteen years? Did he think it not qualified for publication—or was there a deeper reason for the delay?

I think there was. In 1884 Conrad was young enough to be embarrassed by a perceptive reader's divining from that story (as from a dream) its author's secret aspirations and most private perplexities; while in 1924 Conrad was old enough to want to be understood and to let the early story be read for the revelations it might contain concerning the motives and the meaning of his later work. It was as though with the publication of THE BLACK MATE Conrad at long last disclosed the problem which his lifetime of creative writing had been an attempt to solve.

The story has to do with a man whose hair has turned gray while he is yet young. His name is Winston Bunter and he possesses a certificate which entitles him to a position as first mate on any ship. His prematurely gray hair however makes him look too old for the job, and every captain to whom he applies for a first mate's berth rejects him. Bunter finally hits upon a ruse which disguises his disability: he dyes his hair black—and promptly succeeds in landing a job as chief mate for Captain Johns, commander of a ship which travels between London and Calcutta. Bunter's gray hair is not a true disability; it merely places him under an unfair disadvantage in that it causes prospective employers to over-estimate his age. By all truly relevant measuring devices such as chronological age, experience, and official license, Bunter deserves acceptance in the fraternity of ships' officers, but the use of a deceptive convention to exclude him from his rightful status forces him to resort to deception in counterattack.

A storm at sea smashes the bottles of hair-dye, thus threatening Bunter with exposure since his hair will grow out white again weeks before the ship reaches a port where a fresh supply of dye can be secured. His anxieties over the approaching crisis are heightened by an idiosyncrasy of Captain Johns': a habit of discoursing for long hours on spiritualism and spook-lore. The pressure of these two afflictions, Captain Johns' boring monologues on the existence of ghosts and the certainty of the return of his white hair, so unnerve Bunter that he loses his footing on a ladder, falls and gets a head-wound. But while he convalesces in his cabin he lights upon another ruse which he hopes will be as successful in enabling him to retain his status as ship's officer as his first one had been in enabling him to achieve that status.

When he emerges from his cabin, his head-wound cured but his hair now white, he tells Captain Johns that the reason he had fallen from the ladder was that he had seen a ghost, and furthermore that the terror instilled in him by the sight of the ghost had turned his hair white. The ruse works. Captain Johns is joyful for this living proof of the existence of ghosts. He has never seen any ghosts himself, to his sorrow, but now he possesses a man whose white hair

is visible testimony to the fact of their existence, a vindi-
cation of his spiritualistic beliefs, and a weapon with which
to confound the skeptics.

When the ship reaches port, Bunter is not fired as he
had feared but is triumphantly ushered about by Captain
Johns, exhibited as evidence of supernatural presences on
earth. Bunter has, by a ruse, turned his disability into an
asset, thereby making secure his membership in the group
to which he had for so long in vain sought admittance. Both
the disability and the asset were mythological, since the white
hair betokened neither old age nor terror of ghosts but were
erroneously considered to indicate these things by irrational
persons who also possessed the power either to exclude
Bunter from or to establish him in the group to which he
desired admittance.

Bunter's problem was that of proving that he in fact
possessed the youth which his white hair apparently belied.
He had been unjustly condemned, by the stereotype that
gray hair indicates old age, to exclusion from the group
to which he rightfully belongs. The means by which he removes the stigma of old age from his white hair merely sub-
stitutes in place of the false stigma another and more praise-
worthy, though equally false, concept. The superstition that
great fright sometimes turns a person's hair white in a single
night was peculiarly fitted to Bunter's needs in this instance
because of the specific nature of Captain Johns' aberration.
The irrationality of the powers that governed his destiny, the
irresponsibility of the custodians guarding the ships-officers'
membership-lists, forced Bunter to invent invalid grounds to
supplement the valid one entitling him to a seat in the
executive society.

In a sense, society had posed him a pseudo-problem and
so he gave it a pseudo-answer. In itself his white hair was
neither a disability nor an asset but became one or the other
only by reason of the intellectual puerility of persons in po-

sitions of authority. Stripping his problem of particulars and retaining only its universals, one may describe it as belonging to that universe of discourse which deals with the relation of the individual to the group. The qualifications of an individual for group membership, and of the group for meriting an individual's adherence to it, constitute the basic issues raised to view by ths story.

Chapter 2.

ALMAYER'S FOLLY

CONRAD'S FIRST published work was a short novel named ALMAYER'S FOLLY, printed in 1895. Unlike Winston Bunter of THE BLACK MATE, who succeeded in entering and retaining his position in that segment of the social order to which he aspired, Kaspar Almayer of ALMAYER'S FOLLY failed so utterly to attain his ambitions, which were also social, that he ended as an outcast with whom no one would associate except an opium-ravaged Chinaman named Jim-Eng. The handicaps of the two men were alike in that they were fictitious, except for the reality conferred on them by credulous people; they were unlike however in their effects on the two men in that Bunter knew his handicaps to be adventitious while Almayer believed his to be real.

Almayer's one great ambition in life is to make a fortune in the Dutch East Indies so large that it would enable him to compel the aristocratic society of his home country, Holland, to accept and even do homage to his half-breed daughter Nina. The consuming passion with which he desired the stamp of social acceptance in spite of his act of miscegenation caused him to overreach himself to such an extent that he defeated his own purposes. The risks he ran ostensibly to gain wealth for his daughter but in fact merely to salve his own conscience were so great that he lost both daughter and wealth, and the miscalculations which ruined him were rooted in his guilt-feelings at having married a

Sulu woman, native of Borneo. His judgment is under-
mined by his overweening ambition, which in itself was
brought into being by the guilt feelings that he admitted
not even to himself. Almayer wanted to force re-entry for
himself and daughter into society beyond the pale of which
he felt his marriage to a Sulu woman had cast him. It was
Almayer's own belief in the irrational taboo against miscegenation that gave rise to his feeling of estrangement from
society.

The circumstances under which he had become married
to the colored woman, furthermore, had re-enforced rather
than mitigated his middle-aged dismay at his youthful in-
discretion. He had married her for money. She was a Sulu
Sultan's granddaughter, who had been found as a baby girl
by an English sea-captain, Tom Lingard, in the bottom of
a pirate prau all of whose other occupants had been killed
in battle. Captain Lingard had placed the child in a con-
vent, educated her, and when she became of age offered her
in marriage to Almayer, an accountant in a Dutch East
Indies firm, agreeing at the same time to make Almayer his
partner in a trading post and sole heir to his not inconsid-
erable capital accumulations.

The bribe however had subsequently melted away. Captain Lingard's fortune had disappeared in the bankruptcy
of the firm in whose stock the money was invested, and the
lucrativeness of the trading post in Borneo had been destroyed by Arab competition. Lingard had disappeared in
England while attempting to raise capital to develop a gold
mine which he had discovered on an expedition into the
interior of Borneo. At the time the story opens, only three
possessions are left to the almost destitute Almayer: a beautiful half-breed daughter Nina now of marriageable age, a
rough map of Lingard's showing the approximate location
of the gold mine, and a partly completed pretentious house
named "Almayer's Folly" begun in more prosperous past

times on a river in Borneo. Nina's mother has reverted to her native ways and lives in a hut near her white husband's residence.

Almayer has reached a desperate period in his life. He somehow connects the ruin of his financial ambitions with his marriage to a native Bornean woman and he feels that he is despised not only by both brown and white people but by Providence itself for his miscegenation. But he feels too that rescue is possible for him through his daughter Nina who, having been educated in an English school in India and having boarded and roomed in an English family home there, dresses and talks like a member of the white race. Almayer's past life will be vindicated and his violation of the taboo against inter-racial marriage will be effaced, he thinks, if he can become so wealthy that the high society of his home country, Holland, will welcome Nina as a rich European heiress.

His one chance to achieve this is to find the Lingard gold mine. Since he is without funds with which to finance an expedition in search of the mine, he decides to take an illegal and desperate risk. A young Malay prince named Dain Maroola who is promoting a revolt against the Dutch approaches Almayer with an offer of a high price for any guns and ammunition which Almayer can arrange to have smuggled to him in some English tramp steamer. Almayer agrees to do so on the condition that Dain lead an expedition into the interior of Borneo in search of the gold mine.

During his negotiations with Almayer Dain catches sight of Nina and falls in love with her. Almayer's wife, who comes of a royal Malay family as does Dain, secretly and without Almayer's knowledge arranges for love trysts between her daughter and Dain. Almayer notices nothing, because he thinks of Nina as a white girl who could not possibly feel a romantic interest in a colored man, royal or plebeian. Nina, however, secretly prefers to think of herself as a Malay and although she is fond of her father she does not intend to become the instrument by means of which he regains his self-respect in his white world. She loves Dain.

The crisis occurs when a Dutch gunboat runs down and beaches the boat on which Dain is transporting to a place of hiding the shipload of ammunition which Almayer has secured for him. Dain escapes the Dutch but does not want to return to his own land, which lies at some distance from that part of Borneo where Almayer lives, without taking Nina with him. Nina agrees to flee with him but Almayer discovers them together and, horrified at Nina's defection, attempts to persuade her to stay. When she refuses, Almayer attempts to detain her by force—but at that moment the Dutch marines arrive to arrest Dain.

Almayer has an opportunity to choose between two alternatives: he can let the Dutch arrest Dain and find Nina with him, or he can assist both Dain and Nina to escape. In agony, he makes the latter choice, his motive being that he cannot face what he feels would be the disgrace of becoming known as the white man whose daughter was caught eloping with a colored suitor. The last evidence he sees of Nina is the footprints she leaves in the sand as she runs off with Dain, and Almayer gets down on his hands and knees and scoops handfuls of sand with which he builds little mounds like miniature tombs over the footprints.

No need remains for Dain to return and carry out his end of the bargain in helping Almayer to locate the gold, since the use to which Almayer had meant to put the gold has disappeared with Nina's rejection of him. Almayer feels that his only hope of righting himself in the eyes of those whom he deems his peers, the white people of his homeland, has vanished. Nina, the tangible fruit of his transgression, was to have become the instrument of his redemption, but her decision to cast her lot with her mother's colored race rather than with her father's white one sentenced Almayer to spend the remainder of his life shackled to his self-condemnation, spurious though it was. His own belief in the vainglorious myth of race superiority has destroyed him—and separated him from each of the several social groups in which he might have found a home.

Chapter 3.

AN OUTCAST OF THE ISLANDS

IN TELLING the story of Peter Willems (AN OUTCAST OF THE ISLANDS, 1896) Conrad takes a considerably deeper plunge into the problem of the relation between the individual and the social group. The complexity of the question proposed for solution is enormously enlarged in this, Conrad's third, presentation of it. It is as though his explorations of two somewhat related aspects of the problem in his studies of Bunter and Almayer had opened to Conrad's view a wholly new area in which the selfsame problem although in a somewhat transformed guise flourished with even greater vigor.

Whereas Bunter and Almayer seek the approval of a social group, Willems on the other hand is an individualist who in the process of securing the satisfaction of his personal needs runs afoul of a number of such groups and is badly mauled by them. His insouciance of temperament and above-average abilities enable him to effect entry into several groups with much less apparent effort than was required of Bunter and Almayer, but Willems is overtaken by disaster again and again because he underestimates the punitive and coercive power of the social group. He establishes relations with other persons without fully realizing that those persons belong to coherent groups and consequently his ensuing involvement with those groups surprises and shocks him. His interpersonal relations grow, before he is aware of what is happening, into group relations—with the inevitable and repeated result that Willems the individualist finds himself engaged in conflict with overwhelming forces. His unexpected encounters with the social group so unnerve him that he resorts to panic-stricken behavior and thereby comes to grief.

Four times Willems repeats this pattern in his life. The first time, as a boy-apprentice on a Dutch ship from Holland, he becomes a deserter in a Dutch East Indies port. Captain Tom Lingard finds him wandering on the docks in despair because of his unpopularity with the other members of the ship's crew. He takes pity on Willems and gives him a job on his own ship. Willems soon becomes unhappy on this ship as well and so Captain Lingard gets him a clerk's job in the office of a shipping firm in Macassar.

Some years later Captain Lingard again finds Willems wandering on the same docks as before, this time in despair because he has just been fired from his clerk's job for embezzling the firm's funds. Willems had advanced in his position, had married a half-breed native girl whose natural father was the owner of the shipping firm, and had succeeded in secretly returning nearly all of the embezzled funds at the time his theft was discovered. Soon after his marriage, swarms of his wife's relatives had descended on him and it was in order to support them that he had resorted to filching small sums from his employer. Over the years this shortage in his accounts had grown to a very large figure before it began to shrink by means of piecemeal restitutions out of his growing salary. The novel begins with a description of Willems' elation at the knowledge that in a few short weeks his accounts will at long last again be in balance and the weight of his embezzlement lifted from his mind. Discovery and dismissal occur however at the last moment and the bitterness of his disgrace is topped off by the contemptuous attitude displayed toward him by those very relatives who had been the beneficiaries of his embezzlements

and by the refusal of his wife to accompany him on a removal
to another part of the Dutch East Indies for a fresh start in
life.

Rejected and cast out by the very group whose demands
on him had pressed his moral fibre past the breaking point,
Willems feels suicidal. But Captain Lingard rescues him a
second time, takes him several days' journey by sea to a
trading post far up a rocky river in Borneo, the channel of
which is known only to Captain Lingard. This channel is a
jealously guarded secret of his, because the difficulty of navi-
gating the river excludes competitors from access to the
trading area where the Captain possesses, with his partner
Almayer, a very lucrative trading post. (The events of AN
OUTCAST OF THE ISLANDS are chronologically ante-
cedent to those recounted in ALMAYER'S FOLLY.) Willems is left at the post as Almayer's guest while Captain Lingard goes away on what he estimates will be a six weeks'
cruise in search of another shore job for Willems.

The six weeks' absence of Lingard's stretch out however
to nearly as many months, and during that time Willems
repeats, in essence, the pattern which has become recurrent
in his life. He establishes a relation with one person and soon
finds himself embroiled in unforeseen relations with the
social group to which that person belongs; the combined
pressures brought to bear on him by the person and the
group become so great that he permits himself to be maneu-
vered into committing an act injurious to his benefactor and
to his own self-esteem. This act draws him into the orbit of
a much larger human community, the brown race of Southeast Asia, which he finally realizes is attempting to use him
as an instrument in its warfare on the society to which, by
cultural inheritance and color of his skin, he belongs.

The person by whom Willems is drawn into collision with
these social groups is Aissa, a beautiful but half-savage native
girl, daughter of blind Omar, a sea-raider who had lost his

eyesight in his last battle with sailors of the white race. When the Malay chieftains observe the intensity of Willems' passion for Aissa, they persuade Aissa to deny herself to Willems until he agrees to reveal to them the secret channel which Lingard has charted up the river from the sea to the trading post. This would enable one of their own race to establish a rival trading post and ruin the business now carried on as a monopoly by the white men, Almayer and Lingard.

Aissa agrees to carry out her part of the plot because she too hates the white race, members of which had blinded her father. She dreams of inciting her white lover Willems to become a leader of her brown race in a war against the Dutch, thus freeing her people from their colonial overlords. She therefore makes herself inaccessible to Willems and sends him the ultimatum. Until he pilots Abdullah's ship up the river, he can see her only in the presence of Lakamba, the Malay chieftain, in whose house she has taken residence as a guest. She tells him that his reward for revealing the river channel will be partnership with Abdullah as rival trader to Almayer and Lingard and the possession of her, Aissa, as his wife.

Willems writhes in desperate aversion not so much against the act of treachery to his benefactor Captain Lingard as against his personal relation with Aissa becoming a pawn in the power struggle between two social groups, the Malay and the Dutch. He pleads with Aissa to leave Borneo with him so that the two of them can start a new life together soemwhere else, but she refuses as resolutely to part from her social group as Willems' half-breed wife in Macassar had refused to part from hers. So once again Willems is finally driven to a nefarious deed in the service of a group to which not he but a person whom he desires renders allegiance.

He pilots Abdullah's ship up the river, and receives a

stock of supplies with which to set up as a trader in partnership with Abdullah and a sum of money for blind Omar to legitimate the union with Aissa. During the six weeks which then elapse before the arrival of Lingard, Willems becomes progressively more and more aware of, and oppressed by, the role in which Aissa has cast him. The venom with which she humiliates Almayer sickens him, not because he has any sympathetic fellow feeling for Almayer but because he perceives that Aissa's and Almayer's hatred of each other is not personal but a mere function of their feeling of identification with their respective groups. Willems begins to see that it is group loyalty, the patriot impulse itself, that he himself hates, and he becomes more and more uncomfortable with the knowledge that Aissa and her people consider him to be their champion against the whites. His behavior turns secretive and morose in Aissa's presence and less and less cooperative with the Malay chieftains who soon sense his inclination to reject absorption into their group life. They decide that the full extent of Willems' power to serve them had been completed with his exposure of the Lingard river-channel and that he can now be dispensed with.

When Captain Lingard finally arrives on the scene, the Malay chieftains convey to him their acquiescence in any vengeance he may wish to wreak upon Willems, and Willems voluntarily goes to take his merited beating at Lingard's hands, asking only that Lingard take him away from Borneo. Lingard however confounds them all by wrathfully sentencing Willems to life imprisonment on Borneo, captive to the Malays and Aissa. Panic-stricken as though with claustrophobia, Willems presently attempts an escape, secretly aided by Almayer who fears Willems' rivalry and by Willems' wife who had come with Lingard to take her husband back home to Macassar; but Aissa discovers him in flight and kills him.

Having begun his adult life with desertion from one group, a ship's crew, Willems ends his life with another desertion, this time from the Malay community into which he had been drawn by his passion for Aissa. He is the inveterate individualist, to whom the phenomenon of group solidarity is incomprehensible, and whom any group with which he collides inevitably punishes without either regret or mercy. He arrived at his outcast status not by electing to fight any group, nor by his embezzlement, nor even by his treachery to Lingard, but by his inability or refusal to recognize the fact that groups exist and have power over men. It was Willems' innocence and naiveté that defeated him, and his assumption that a strictly personal and private life is possible in a world of organized social groups. Failing to take the fact of group life into account, he neglected to provide himself with means of defence against the encroachments of the group and therefore became the agent of his own defeat. Deficient in group feeling himself, he underestimated its strength as his antagonist and the force of its magnetic power over other individuals.

Chapter 4.

THE NIGGER OF THE NARCISSUS

EACH OF the first three men whose predicaments, as presented by Conrad, we have analyzed so far were individuals in conflict with society. Their personal problems can be localized in that area of their lives where relations with social groups are carried on, and in one fashion or another each of the three men is at odds with the social group or groups with which he comes in contact. Bunter is at first excluded from the social group to which he wishes to belong, and after he effects entry into it he stands in danger of being thrown out. Almayer's conflict with society occurs introspectively, since his problem has to do with a discrepancy between his actual behavior in a Bornean residence and his idea of the kind of behavior that would be required of a man in good standing in his home country, Holland. Willems attempts to ignore society, but society takes the initiative and enters into conflict with him.

The fourth man whose story Conrad tells us, James Wait (THE NIGGER OF THE NARCISSUS, 1897), adopts an attitude towards the outcast role very different from that taken by the above three men. Wait chooses the outcast role on his own initiative and shrewdly exploits the unfair advantages which can be wrung from it by an adroit individual. He turns it into a weapon against the social group, and he succeeds very well with it for a time. Wait was not a true outcast, however, but an actor, a fakir and a fraud, and his weapon finally turns on him like a boomerang and kills him.

The social group which James Wait nearly succeeds in demoralizing and disrupting is the crew of the ship "Narcissus," headed by Captain Allistoun. The first thing about Wait that sets him apart from the group is the color of his skin: he is a negro. Secondly, he possesses a magnificent voice, far superior in timbre and quality to that of any other man on the ship. Thirdly, his large size and powerful physique make his strength double that of an ordinary man. By virtue of his voice, physique and color, Wait stands out separated from the group as though by natural endowment. Furthermore, his speech and manners are those of a man possessing an education far superior to that of the other crew members.

From the day he comes on board the ship in Bombay until the day he dies, just before the ship reaches London, Wait manages to keep the entire crew of twenty-five men in a state of perpetual psychological crisis. Even his death seems to be a histrionic achievement, after he has held the center of the stage as though by natural right during the entire voyage. He captures the attention of all on board and retains it, fixed upon himself, at such cost to the ship's discipline that Captain Allistoun all but loses command of his own men.

The method Wait utilizes to acquire outcast status is that of inciting the ship's officers to take punitive disciplinary measures against him which he then succeeds in making appear to be excessively harsh in the eyes of his fellow sailors. He thus becomes the focal point for a tug of war between the ship's crew and the ship's officers. The officers, in the interest of discipline and order, do not dare relax their punitive attitude towards Wait, and the crew cannot, with honor, idly stand by and permit one of their fellow sailors to be persecuted. Wait impales the sailors on their sense of honor and fair play, on that element in universal human nature which sentimentally springs to the defense of a victim of injustice, especially when that victim can contrive to make himself appear to be a symbol standing for the multiple ways in which all persons feel themselves victimized by those in power over them. He enacts a masterly paradox in that he plays the part of a victim so convincingly that he victimizes everyone within his reach.

His first act on board ship wins not only everybody's attention but their sympathy and concern as well: he produces a seemingly uncontrollable bad fit of coughing. And when they hear his educated speech and modulated beautiful voice and notice his good manners, their sympathy and concern are reënforced by genuine respect for this black man. Wait is too great a master, however, in the technique of keeping attention centered upon himself to let any one emotional attitude towards him remain undisturbed for long. His next act is to anger the men by not doing his share of the work. When he has them roused to the point of complaining of it to him, he uses his magnificent voice to shame them for speaking that way to a sick man, pointing to his throat and producing another terrifying fit of coughing so severe that it seems to shatter his great frame. A few days later, when the chief mate scolds him for his indolence, Wait advances a stronger argument: he says that he is dying. Baker, the mate, takes this for insolence and orders him to his quarters. The sailors somewhat resent Baker's harshness with Wait, and yet they also think that Wait "had it coming."

Baker does not permit Wait to return to work, and so Wait lies in bed most of the time. When the sailors laugh too loud, Wait scolds them for making so much noise in the presence of a dying man. They are abashed and quiet down, looking at one another guiltily. One of the sailors, named Belfast, steals a pie out of the kitchen behind the cook's back and gives it to Wait. The disappearance of the pie annoys the cook, Podmore, very much. He is a religious man and he quotes scripture at the crew, accusing them of thievery and deploring the general breakdown of morality. They are all very ill at ease and resent Podmore's accusations.

⟋ When Wait objects to a wet deck, saying that it aggravates his cough and further weakens him, the sailors almost mutiny against the mate's orders to swab down the deck as usual. Discipline on the ship threatens to disintegrate because of the crew's reaction to the presence on the ship of that big, handsome, lazy, sick "nigger." The mate finally sends Wait to Captain Allistoun's cabin, thereby placing on the Captain's shoulders the responsibility of deciding whether Wait is merely lazy or really sick.

The captain decides that it doesn't make any difference whether it's laziness or sickness: the man is a total loss anyway as a working seaman. He gives orders that a small shelter be erected for Wait on the deck—to keep him away from the other seamen. But this doesn't help at all, because the men spend their off-duty time visiting Wait in his shelter, discussing him and the way the officers are treating him.

Opinions about Wait range all the way from one extreme, represented by Belfast who thinks Wait is a dying man and should be treated tenderly, to the other extreme represented by Donkin who thinks that Wait is a fakir, that he has been smart enough to discover a sure dodge to keep out of the way of hard work while continuing to draw his pay. Belfast is a good, hard-working seaman, while Donkin is a lazy ne'er-do-well. Donkin both admires and is jealous of Wait; he would like to be as successful a malingerer. A natural troublemaker, however, he conceals his real opinion of Wait from the crew and stirs them up to rebellious feelings against the officers because of their harsh treatment of a sick man. Belfast, although he does not have a mutinous temperament, cannot counteract Donkin's bad effect on the morale of the men. Belfast believes in Wait's sickness and has to admit that everything Donkin says is true. Everyone's nerves are on edge because of the uncertainty as to whether or not James Wait is a fraud.

At this point a gale strikes the ship and turns it over on its side. The entire crew, including the captain, clings to the vertically sloping deck for about sixty hours. After the storm subsides they are able to set a sail and slowly bring the ship again to an upright position. The accident puts the Wait problem out of everybody's mind for a few hours— until someone suddenly notices that Wait's shelter is nearly submerged and the door itself under water. A few men risk their lives crawling to the shelter; they chop a hole in its unsubmerged side, find Wait swimming around on the water within a foot of the top side, and pull him out by the hair.

About this time, a third opinion about James Wait makes its appearance. Singleton, the carpenter, an old man with a beard, announces that Wait is a "jinx" and that the good ship "Narcissus" will never make port until Wait dies. He also maintains a thesis that the storm and near-disaster were brought about by Wait's presence on the ship.

Podmore, the religious cook, tries to convert Wait. He spends hours in Wait's shelter exhorting him to accept the true religion before he dies. This enrages Wait who cannot bear these references to his approaching death. Whether or not his sickness had been feigned previous to his soaking in the flooded shelter and his subsequent chill while clinging with the other men to the sloping deck, he is really ill now. However, now that he is scared, he makes a gigantic effort at recovery, pretends to be a well man—and asks Captain Allistoun's permission to return to work. The captain refuses, angered by all the vacillations in Wait's and the other mens' opinions about the sick man's health, but in fact motivated more by pity for the dying man than by anger at all the trouble he has caused. Wait is actually so sick and weak that he can't stand on his feet without support and it is a profoundly kinder act of Allistoun's to order Wait to stay in bed, where his nearness to death will not be so apparent to him, than would be any granting of permission to attempt work beyond his strength to accomplish.

The captain's decision, however, precipitates a near-mutiny on board ship. Some of the sailors interpret Allistoun's order as a cruel denial to a dying man of his last wish, others as an arbitrary assumption on Allistoun's part that Wait had been lying when he said he was sick and is lying now when he says he is well. The entire crew gathers in a milling crowd near Wait's shelter and many of the seamen shout imprecations at the captain. Fights, both physical and verbal, take place here and there in the crowd between small groups upholding various and contradictory courses of action against the officers of the ship. Donkin tries, but fails, to get the men to make a concerted rush to overpower the officers; disappointed in his attempt, he hurls an iron belaying pin at the captain who is on his way back to his cabin after his visit to Wait's shelter.

Into their feelings of resentment at the treatment being meted out to James Wait the seamen pour the pent-up emotions generated by all the other frustrations in their lives. James Wait has become, as Conrad says, "the fit emblem of their aspirations." Donkin's hatred of authority, Belfast's need for a sentimental attachment, Podmore's impulse to proselyte, Singleton's desire for a scapegoat, and the collective crew's want of a focal point at which to exert the rancour aroused by their personal shortcomings and by real or fancied injustices: all these were given release by the James Wait predicament.

The ambiguity of their grievance prevents them from making any organized revolt against their officers' authority, and Captain Allistoun cows them the next morning by assembling them to listen in one body to his speech of castigation. He also walks up to Donkin and hands him the belaying pin, ordering him to put it back where he got it.

During the next few weeks Wait sinks rapidly towards death. The crew, ill at ease, skulk about the decks in shamefaced fascination with the spectacle of Wait's losing battle with death. No one wants him to die, but everyone knows that his death will release them from the unwelcome spell which he has cast over them. Head winds and calm retard the speed of the ship in its progress towards home and exasperatingly prolongs the duration of its crew's nervous tension. Singleton assures them that favorable winds will not come until Wait dies.

Belfast tenderly nurses Wait during those last long weeks, but it happens to be Donkin who is present during Wait's final anguished hours. They occur at the dead of night, while Donkin sits at Wait's bedside taunting him ghoulishly with his approaching death and rifling his trunk of its money and valuables during Wait's struggle with his death rattle. By tyrannizing over and exacting penalties from the helpless Wait, Donkin gets some venomous satisfaction for his discomfiture at failing to incite the sailors to mutiny on Wait's behalf.

After Wait dies and is buried, the men quiet down, the psychological air clears, and the recent feverish excitement over Wait seems to have been a bad dream which has faded away. But Wait had had his way with them nevertheless, even if it had cost him his life. He had learned how to play upon the guilt and resentment feelings of the social group so ably that he achieved virtuoso status as a tyrannizer over the group from which he had succeeded in getting himself cast out. Conrad seems to be saying that the social outcast is a catalytic agent which startles society into realizing that to cast out even one of its members is to render itself vulnerable to disintegration.

Chapter 5.

THE IDIOTS

THREE OF Conrad's first four stories tell of a tussle between an individual and a group, both of which are present in the action, while one (ALMAYER'S FOLLY) tells of a struggle that occurs within a man's mind between two attitudes towards himself, one from his personal autonomous individual point of view and the other from his point of view as a hypothetical member of an absent society (the one home in Holland.) Almayer's torment originates in his conviction that the good people back home would scorn him for his miscegenation. He is ashamed of himself because his daughter is a half-breed.

In Conrad's fifth story, the parents, Jean and Suzan Bacadou, are ashamed of themselves because their four children are idiots, and their torment originates in the conviction that their neighbors must surely scorn them for being unworthy vessels of generation. Neither in ALMAYER'S FOLLY nor in THE IDIOTS (1898) does the group take an active part in the events, but in both stories it is the putative opinions ascribed to the absent society by the stories' characters that determines those characters' actions and their attitudes towards themselves. They look at themselves through the eyes of their group—and find themselves wanting.

Jean Bacadou, a French peasant who owns his land, marries the daughter of a good family, Susan Levaille. Their first children are twin boys, and Jean looks forward happily to the time when he can pass on to his sons the land which his own father had passed on to him. After a few months, however, he discovers that the twins are idiots and will be forever useless. This great disappointment nearly unnerves Jean, weighs Suzan down with a sense of guilt, and makes both of them feel ashamed before their neighbors.

Suzan's next child proves to be a boy too, and both Jean and Suzan anxiously watch the baby grow, feverishly hoping that he will turn out to be a normal child. But their hopes are soon dashed: this child, too, is an idiot. In his despair, Jean turns to the Church, renounces his previous anti-clericalism and becomes a devout Catholic. He thinks that perhaps the three idiot children are punishments visited on him from heaven for his atheism and that his conversion to religion will remove the curse and permit Suzan to reward him with a fourth child who will be healthy and strong like his neighbor's children.

An idiot girl arrives, however, to confound Jean's hypothesis concerning the cause of his misfortune. In the violence of his rage at this fourth indignity, Jean takes to drink, reviles the Church, beats his wife, and lets his land go to ruin. He feels utterly dishonored by a cruel and undeserved fate and becomes more anti-clerical than he had ever been in his early youth, thinking now that the priests have tricked and deluded him with false promises.

Appalled by their growing brood of idiots, Jean and Suzan impose sexual abstinence on themselves for a time. Jean, however, soon tires of the severity of this regimen and suggests to Suzan that they try once more to produce a normal child. Jean can reconcile himself neither to the ascetic life nor to the prospect of relinquishing his land, when he dies, into the hands of anyone other than a son of his own. But Suzan refuses to have any more children. When Jean attempts to force her, she is so overcome by the dread and horror of bringing another idiot into the world that she stabs her stubborn husband in the throat with a scissors, killing him.

Terrified at what she has done, she dashes out into the dark night and runs wildly along the seashore. A strange man sees her and gives chase, thinking that she is some loose woman desiring pursuit and capture. In her hysteria and delirium, Suzan imagines the strange man to be the ghost of her husband, returned from beyond death itself to reiterate his demands upon her. Her despair impels her at last to leap from a cliff into the sea, where she drowns.

Jean and Suzan are crushed by shame. The ignominy of exposure to all the world, through their offspring, as being carriers of the seeds of idiocy drives them on to destruction. Their sense of guilt, since it is irremediable, goes deeper than Almayer's. He had at least a chance, so he thought, to retrieve his lost honor; but Jean's and Suzan's idiot children live on, in full view of the neighbors, as an ever-present proof of their parents' turpitude. Jean and Suzan stand convicted in their own eyes of being defective links in the social chain and they feel the disgrace of it so deeply that only tragic death can extinguish their pain.

Chapter 6.

AN OUTPOST OF PROGRESS

THE IDIOTS was followed by THE OUTPOST OF PROGRESS, which is built on the same basic theme as THE IDIOTS and ALMAYER'S FOLLY. All three tell the stories of people who destroy themselves because they feel that they have not lived up to the standards held in esteem by the social group of which they deem themselves to be members, and also in all three stories the social group is present in the action only in spirit, its influence reaching from Europe to Almayer in Borneo and from Europe to the heart of Africa in THE OUTPOST OF PROGRESS.

The last-named story adds a new touch to the theme of interrelatedness between individuals and groups in that Conrad for the first time seems to give particular attention to the injurious effect which physical separation from the group inflicts upon the individual's sense of security. Neither Almayer nor Willems, for instance, is described as being consciously disturbed by the physical absence from his immediate surroundings of the social group into which he had been born. Kayerts and Carlier, on the other hand, in THE OUTPOST OF PROGRESS (1898), feel very acutely the loss of support from their social surroundings which removal from their European homes to an African trading post had cost them. All four men gradually change from persons who are merely living apart from their group, in a foreign land, to persons whose actions in those places where the social surveillance of their group is inoperative impel them to stigmatize themselves as transgressors, meriting social outcast status. They sit in judgment on themselves, render a verdict of "guilty," and pass sentence. They feel unfit to rejoin their respective groups, and die in exile.

The two Europeans, Kayerts and Carlier, had intended to spend only a few years in Africa. They had been tempted by the high commissions paid by an importer of African ivory into accepting his offer to send them deep into Africa to take charge of one of his trading posts. The commission rate offered them on the volume of ivory already flowing through that station would in a few short years of residence make them independently rich, and moreover their principal duty would be merely to live in the importer's buildings there already in existence, eat and sleep at the importer's expense, and keep watch on the natives who are now operating the trading post. Their only labor will be to post to ledger sheets the count of beads going out to, and of ivory tusks coming in from, the native tribesmen. They will be living three hundred miles distant from the nearest white man, and the ship which brings the beads and removes the ivory will be calling on them only once in six months, but they will have unlimited leisure, free food and lodging, and each other for company. It seems to them that a few short years out of their lives spent apart from their friends and associates will be a small price to pay for the great financial rewards which will accrue to their account in an European bank.

When they arrive at the post, after a long journey by river-boat into mid-Africa, they find that it is staffed by about ten black men supervised by a tri-lingual and civilized black man named Makola. All the duties and responsibilities of managing the post are being competently performed by Makola, who is even doing the bookkeeping which was to have been Kayert's and Carlier's sole occupation. Since Makola also carries on the negotiations with the savages who bring in the ivory for sale, there is little left

for Kayerts and Carlier to do but watch Makola do their
work.

All goes well with them for a few months. Gobila, chief
of a neighboring savage tribe, pays an occasional visit to
the post, sits with Kayerts and Carlier and exchanges friendly
gestures and grimaces with them, and sees to it that his
subjects bring in quantities of ivory whether they are in
need of beads or not. The two white men are bothered by
occasional qualms of conscience when they think of the
infinitesimal value of the glass beads which are given to the
negroes in exchange for their immensely valuable ivory;
but they are able to suppress the qualms quite easily when
they calculate the commissions which will be due them
from their Company upon arrival of the ivory in Europe.

Then, one morning about five months after their arrival
at the post, they are startled by the sudden and unexpected
appearance on the scene of a wandering band of native
warriors from some distant tribe. They camp near the
station grounds and stay for several days. Kayerts and Carlier
are worried by the unfriendly arrogance of the strangers.
After nightfall sounds of shouting and revelry fill the air,
and an occasional rifle-shot rings out. Gobila tells the scared
white men that the visitors are drinking liquor but that he
expects to be able to keep them from getting too rowdy.
He also asks for permission to distribute some palm wine
among the native workmen at the post, since they are eager
to join in the revelry over at the strangers' camp.

During the ensuing night, both the gang of native
workers and the band of warriors disappear, but the next
morning there are six magnificent tusks of ivory in the station yard. Under questioning by Kayerts, Makola finally
admits that he had sold the workers into slavery to the warriors, in exchange for the ivory. Kayerts and Carlier are appalled, because they feel that by this transaction their deputy
Makola has forced upon them the role of slave dealer. For

a time they refuse to accept the ivory, hoping thereby to evade responsibility for their deputy's reprehensible act. But when they see the hot sun beginning to injure the ivory, they help Makola store it away in the warehouse alongside the legitimately acquired ivory; and it is not long before both Kayerts and Carlier are including the contraband tusks in the inventory total on which they calculate their commissions.

Gobila's visits cease after this, and his continued absence is interpreted by the two white men as indicating that he and all his tribe are shunning them because they are slave dealers. They begin to feel like accomplices in crime rather than devoted friends. They become irritable and begin to quarrel over small matters. Their supplies are running low, because they had not been replenished for over eight months. The steamer which had brought Kayerts and Carlier up the river to the trading post had been due to return in six months with fresh supplies, but it is already two months late.

The combination of stale food, slight attacks of tropical fever, solitude, and bad conscience finally overcomes both men. They quarrel hysterically over the last of the sugar. The quarrel turns into a fight—and Kayerts kills Carlier with a revolver. Makola suggests that they pretend to the authorities that Carlier had died of fever. Kayerts agrees—but does not succeed in getting the dead man buried and out of the way before the arrival of the steamer. The repeated whistles of the approaching boat strike such terror into him that he hangs himself while the passengers are coming ashore.

Kayerts and Carlier succumbed under the weight of the "white man's burden." The price they were paying for the financial gain had turned out to be too great to be borne, since it gradually dawned on them that they had allowed themselves to be drawn into becoming participants in a great predatory swindle which not only separated them from the black men of Africa but would, if the truth were known, alienate them from their former friends and associates back home in Europe. Furthermore, each of the two men knew that the other despised him for acquiescing in what seemed to both of them to be the gaining of ivory and riches by virtual theft. Acceptance of the ivory procured by Makola's selling the station's employees into slavery merely sharpened the point of the thorn already digging into their flesh: their vague feeling of guilt at trading worthless glass beads for priceless ivory tusks. It offended the practises of fair-dealing to which they had become accustomed in their European social surroundings, and they felt that they had inadvertently consented to participate in practices which were reprehensible according to the code of honorable conduct subscribed to by the social group to which they belonged. They really felt that they had forfeited their rights of membership in their own community in Europe and would therefore be forever unable to enjoy the riches which were accumulating to their account in European banks.

Their fate is similar to that of Almayer's, and of Jean and Suzan Bacadou's, in that all five of them feel that something in themselves has broken faith with the group to which they belong by birth and they consequently cannot find the heart with which to go on living. Willems was destroyed by the group because of his deficiency in group feeling; James Wait destroyed himself by making an illegitimate bid for the coddling treatment sometimes measured out by the group to its maimed members; and Bunter the "black mate" had been forced to resort to crafty strategems to induce the group to grant privileges which had, by reason of irrational prejudices on the part of the group, been wrongfully withheld from him. All of these stories have to do with the inter-relationship of the individual and the group, and they vary only in the direction from which the approach is made to this area of experience.

Chapter 7.

KARAIN: A MEMORY

IN EACH one of the six stories considered up to this point, the concept of guilt in one form or another enters strongly into the total picture of the leading characters as presented by Conrad. The ship captains to whom Bunter applied for a mate's position thought him guilty of asking for a job for which he was over-age. Almayer felt himself guilty of some wrong-doing because he had married a colored woman in order to become Lingard's partner and heir. Willems was considered guilty by his wife's relatives of having disgraced them by being exposed as an embezzler, by his employer for having embezzled, by Captain Lingard for having betrayed his secret river-channel to the Malays, by the Malays for not energetically and enthusiastically performing his duties as a trader in partnership with Abdullah, and by Aissa for attempting to desert her instead of helping her to lead the Malays in a war on the Dutch. The men of the Narcissus spent most of their time during a voyage lasting several months disputing among themselves as to whether or not James Wait was guilty of malingering. Jean and Susan Bacadou felt themselves to be guilty of some biological defect in their capacity as procreative organisms. And Kayerts and Carlier were guilt-struck at finding themselves to be helpless beneficiaries of a pattern of colonial exploitation which outraged their naive sensibilities and preconceptions.

In his seventh story, KARAIN: A MEMORY (1898), Conrad comes to closer grips with the concept of guilt. Un-

like the above-named persons, who feel that a social group
is pointing the finger of guilt at them or that they as members of such a group are pointing the finger of guilt at themselves, Karain on the other hand feels his guilt solely as a
person and without reference to any social group. Karain is
a king, an absolute ruler over his subject group, and is therefore untouchable by group opinion concerning his personal
conduct. It could never occur to Karain that judgment might
be passed on him by anyone but himself—with one exception: a friend whom he had wronged. By creating a character
who by his very nature is beyond the reach of any social
group, Conrad refines to its marrow the specific traumatic
experience that obsesses him. And what this is becomes somewhat clearer by the addition of Karain to Conrad's dramatis
personae.

In his youth, Karain had had a close friend by the name
of Matara, whose sister, although engaged to marry a Malay,
had run off with a red-headed Dutchman. Matara had asked
Karain to accompany him on a search throughout the entire
Malay Peninsula for the guilty pair. It is Matara's duty,
according to Malay tradition, to kill his sister, because she
had broken her marriage contract. Karain goes with Matara
on his search, but he does not want the girl to be found
and killed, because he is in love with her himself. She
appears to him in his dreams and begs him to protect her
from her brother's vengeance.

After several years of wandering, Matara and Karain
finally locate the guilty pair. Karain had promised the girl
in his dreams that he would save her from death, so now
he realizes that he can redeem his promise only by killing
Matara, his best friend. When Matara, knife in hand, springs
at his sister from the ambush in which Karain and he had
been hiding, Karain empties the contents of his rifle, not into
the Dutchman, but into Matara instead.

He had saved the girl's life; but not many days afterwards, as he sits beside a campfire in the forest, he sees Matara coming towards him, walking as though he were alive. Matara sits down beside the astonished Karain and repeats the last words he had spoken in life. In terror, Karain jumps up and runs away; but he flees in vain, because Matara runs easily by his side.

For several years the ghost is Karain's ever-present companion, an afflicting spectre which haunts and harries the conscience-driven Malay. However, an old man, a sorcerer, finally relieves Karain of his ghost. The mere presence of this man serves to exorcize the unwelcome visitant, so Karain keeps him by his side night and day. They travel together, and Karain eventually becomes a great chief, the absolute ruler over a settlement in Mindanao consisting of refugees from Dutch rule in other parts of the Malay Archipelago.

When the old sorcerer dies, however, the ghost of Matara resumes his vigil by Karain's side. Karain tries to escape him by locking himself up alone in a single-roomed hut, but to no avail. He does not emerge from his seclusion even to welcome in his customary manner the officers of the English ship which had arrived with another load of contraband ammunition for him. (Karain, like many other petty Malay chieftains, was forever planning uprisings against the Dutch invaders.) But the night before the ship is due to leave, Karain swims from shore, alone and nearly naked, and clambers up the side of the ship. He tells the astonished Englishmen the story of his life and implores them either to take him away with them or to give him some powerful charm. Matara's ghost can be prevented from materializing by his side in only two ways: by the presence of white unbelievers or by Karain's possession of some dread talisman.

One of the ship's officers remembers that Karain's mother had been a great Queen, and that Karain has always been intensely interested in hearing about the English Queen. So he shows Karain a necklace to which is attached a Jubilee sixpence stamped with the image of Queen Victoria. Karain is immensely struck with the trinket, accepts it at once as the talisman he requires, and goes back to his people a free man, secure in the knowledge that Matara's ghost is gone forever.

This does not mean, however, that the wrong which Karain had committed had been righted; it merely means that he feels provided with a sure defense against suffering the consequences of his guilt. The law which he had not been able to avoid breaking still remains a law to him. He and Matara had formed a group of two, and his killing of Matara in order to protect that other group of two consisting of himself and Matara's sister did nevertheless constitute an irreparable injury to the group of which he and Matara were the sole members. Karain's hallucination, Matara's ghost, personified his grief at having been forced to commit an act which did violence to, and separated him from, the group which he and Matara made.

Chapter 8.

THE RETURN

In CONRAD's next story, THE RETURN (1898), the larger social group which exists in the near background of every person's life re-enters as an influence on the characters whose actions are presented. In the previous stories the social group is, in the eyes of the characters, the unquestioned court of last resort, the final arbiter whose judgment is accepted as though it were a fact of nature which must be adjusted to and lived with. In THE RETURN, however, the chief act of the main character, Alan Hervey, is a virtual declaration of independence from the group, and the implication of Alvan's revolt is that a life lived in accordance with the dictates of the group furnishes merely the appearance of living while a life lived in accordance with one's own personally felt needs will furnish the reality. This story seems to say that to seek the approval of the group may be to find the heavy hand that crushes out the individual life, whereas the previous stories seemed to assume that reconciliation with the group was the source of happiness. THE RETURN comes to the reader of Conrad as a somewhat belated warning from the author that the assumptions implicit in the previous stories will bear some re-examination.

Alvan Hervey had been during his entire life an unprotesting and contented member of his group. He had been married for five years, has supported his wife well, and has lived a conventional and sociable home life. He had been

successful at his work and was now about to be advanced
by his superiors to a higher level of responsibility.

The story opens with Alvan's arriving home from his
office one evening to find a note from his wife informing
him that she has left him and is eloping that very evening
with another man. She had hitherto given him no reason
to suspect that she was unhappy and no forewarning of her
intention to leave him.

The astounding news contained in his wife's note creates
in Alvan a succession of emotions: fear, humiliation, rage,
sadness and desolation. Each of these emotions, however,
springs from his wounded vanity, not one from speculation
on the state of his wife's feelings. His life has been without
reproach up to this point, and scandal in his domestic life
will seriously jeopardize his impending business promotion.
The reader begins to sympathize with the runaway wife and
to suspect that her life with such a selfish husband must
have become intolerable.

About an hour or two after he has read her note, his
wife returns, astounding him a second time. She announces
that she has changed her mind and had turned back before
reaching the rendezvous where her expectant lover waits.
Alvan rages at her for a time, but when she offers to leave
him he asks her to stay. She listens submissively while he
preaches her a sermon consisting mainly of the conventional
clichés of outraged morality. The tenor of his remarks is
far removed from any relevance to the state of her feelings.
When he reaches the point of telling her that he is ready,
from a sense of duty, to forgive her, she bursts into hysterical
laughter, thus astounding him a third time.

They are called to dinner by the maid, and they obey
the summons in order to keep up appearances in front of
the servants. Her composure during the meal mystifies him;
the disparity between her tumultous feelings and her calm
appearance teaches him that he may never be able to arrive

at the truth about his wife. He thereupon decides that, since truth is unattainable, he will turn his attention exclusively to the manageable outward form of visible life. He tells his wife that it is their duty to be a good example to society and that they should continue to live together as though nohing had occurred. He goes on to state received opinions as though they were his own, until finally the sentiments he is expressing begin to sound hollow even to his own ears. His very emphasis on the value of keeping up appearances calls to his attention, as if by contrast, the loss which will be concealed by the appearances he is invoking. For the first time in his life he realizes the importance of the certitude of love and faith, and the comparative unimportance of morality and appearance.

He begins to falter in his rhetoric, hesitating to use his customary stereotyped phrases because they unexpectedly seem now not to carry his intended meaning. Hardly realizing what is happening to him, he seems to be experiencing a shift in his meanings even while he is stating them. The power to feel genuine and personal, as opposed to standardized, emotion is beginning to germinate within him, but the vocabulary with which to express it escapes him. He speaks of love—but lamely, and his wife repels him. When he holds out his arms to her in a mute appeal, she screams the words "this is odious," and runs off to her bedroom.

After an interval, he decides to follow her there but is delayed by the servants who are closing up the house for the night. He spends some minutes considering his wife's remark that he had loved himself but never her and he concludes that this must be taken as proof at least of her complete hostility to him. Her last-minute rejection of the other man and her return home means simply that, not having the courage of her emotions, she fails to possess the gift of love and faith and therefore cannot confer it either upon him or upon any other man. By her decision to return to

him, she had chosen the conventional life of form and structure and rejected the emotional life. She had chosen the
shadow and rejected the substance.

This was exactly the choice that he had been urging upon
her, and he realizes that he will be only concurring in her
choice if he follows her to her room. But something re-
strains him. He has been discovering by himself, even while
engaged in advocating it, that a life without emotional content is no life at all. His wife's decision to return to him
seems to indicate that that kind of life is good enough for
her, but he is beginning to doubt that it is good enough
for him. This is, to him, a revolutionary conception and he
is speedily realizing that if he allows this doubt to become
the point of departure for a new attitude on his part, the
course of his entire life will be altered.

By this time the reader's sympathies have completely re-
versed themselves. We now condemn the runaway wife for
her return to a stillborn marriage, and we ardently favor
the husband in his struggle to make his life conform with
emotional verities rather than with custom and habit. He
goes into his wife's room, asks her if she "can stand it";
upon receiving her affirmative reply, he shouts, "Well, I
can't." He then possesses our entire support when he leaves
the house, never to return.

Conrad here equates the emotional content of a life
with non-conformity to group expectations and his point
would seem to be that emotional reciprocity is the desidera-
tum rather than simply group feeling in itself. In the stories
previous to THE RETURN, a rift between the individual
and the group, even if only imagined, resulted in a loss of
euphoria on the part of the individual, whereas in THE
RETURN euphoria can only be attained by Alvan Hervey
through an affront to the group. In Alvan's case, the disappearance of emotional reciprocity between himself and his
wife as a representative of the group drained from his group-

feeling all the value and worth which it had hitherto held for him, and he therefore changes course and takes the path, apparently with Conrad's full approval, which leads in the direction of social outcast status. Alvan's decision means that he would feel social outcast status to be preferable to a life in which social conformity concealed the lack of, rather than indicated the presence of, a feeling of being at one with the group.

Chapter 9.

THE LAGOON

THE LAGOON (1898) which follows THE RETURN, also tells the story of a man who, with Conrad's apparent approval, revolts from the group. Both Alvan Hervey, a Britisher in London, and Arsat, a Malay in Southeast Asia, find it necessary in their respective ways to affront their social groups in order to free their personal emotional lives from society's smothering hand. The similarity of basic tension in the two stories is not, however, expressed in similar action-patterns, since in the one case social pressure works against the dissolution of a marriage while in the other it works against the occurrence of a marriage. Alvan's need, in the interest of personal fulfillment, is to break out of his marriage, while Arsat's need is to achieve a marriage that society has prohibited. In these two stories, separation from the social group furthers the interests of the individual, while in Conrad's first seven stories it was separation from the group that initiated evils and disasters and death. Conrad's attitude towards the demands of society upon the individual seems to have taken a sharp change of direction.

The difference in tempo between the two stories is very noticeable. It is as though Conrad had slowed down to change his course while writing THE RETURN, and had then returned to full speed ahead in the new direction while writing THE LAGOON. In THE RETURN Conrad subtly places Alvan's foot for its first step on the path which would eventually lead him to a position wherein he would

find himself braving and standing firm against the buffet-
ings of social disapproval, while in THE LAGOON he
makes Arsat take one intentionally violent leap into a position wherein the total society of which he was a member
would not only turn against him but even spring into action
like a pack of wolves in pursuit of prey.

Arsat lived in a Malay state ruled by an autocratic Rajah
who possessed power of life and death over his subjects.
Both he and Diamelen, the girl whom he loves, are employed
in the royal palace, Arsat as sword-bearer to the Rajah,
Diamelen as maid to the Malay Queen. Upon rejection of
his petition that he and Diamelen be granted permission
to leave the employ of the palace, since they wish to marry
and cannot do so in view of the royal prohibition against
marriages among the palace servants, Arsat decides that he
and Diamelen must flee from the Rajah's domains to some
far country. He knows quite well that to carry out this decision will be to become not only a social outcast but an
outlaw as well, because the Rajah will sentence him to be
shot and killed on sight.

Arsat and Diamelen are willing to pay the price of
permanent separation from their social group in order to
obtain something denied them by that social group: possession of each other in marriage. When they take flight, they
are assisted by Arsat's brother. The three of them are pursued by the Rajah's soldiers; Arsat and Diamelen escape,
but the brother is killed. The lovers go to a far country and
live happily for several years. Diamelen, however, then dies
of some malignant fever and Arsat is left alone in the world
while still a young man. He remembers his brother's death
at the hands of the Rajah's soldiers and realizes that the
one remaining personal need yet remaining unsatisfied is
his need to avenge that brother's death. It will be his destiny to return to his native land, kill a half-dozen of the
Rajah's soldiers in payment for his brother's life, and then

die an honorable death in satisfaction of the Rajah's sentence against him.

Arsat's attitude towards life seems to be that of stoical and fatalistic contentment at having been able to meet all the demands which his personal emotional life had lain upon him. These demands had been hard in that they had brought him into conflict with his Rajah and condemned him to exile; and now they require of him that he kill many men and die a violent death. But he will have succeeded in maintaining the keynote of his life: fidelity in carrying out the exactions levied upon him by his emotional attachments and translated by him into obligations owed by an individual to himself.

Arsat and Alvin had each in his separate way asserted the insistent need of the individual for personal and emotional self-fulfillment as taking precedence over the need of the individual for reconciliation with the group. This constituted a new tack for Conrad to take, an abrupt shift in his attitude towards the theme of individual-group interrelations. And we shall see that his next story, YOUTH (1898), is a statement by Conrad upon the subject of this change of attitude towards the one basic problem with which his fiction grapples.

Chapter 10.

YOUTH

WE HAVE seen that Conrad's first seven stories held up to our view persons who were subject, in an exaggerated degree, to the influence exerted on them by their social groups, while his eighth and ninth stories tell of persons who successfully seceded from their social groups. His tenth story (YOUTH) describes the last heroic surge of effort by which the boy Marlowe becomes a man at last. Marlowe expends his youth in the purchase of something more desirable to him than youth: performance on an adult level, just as Conrad had spent a decade in achieving something which he felt it had been worth a decade of his life to achieve: a maturity of attitude toward the phenomenon of individual-group interrelations. By working his way through the situations presented in his first nine stories, Conrad had forged for himself an adult point of view towards, and therefore some degree of freedom from, the problem which had seized him.

The outstanding difference between YOUTH and all the stories preceding it is that its main character, Marlowe, is the chief executive of a group, while the main characters of the preceding stories are ex-members of a group. The shift in point of view from Winston Bunter of THE BLACK MATE to Marlowe of YOUTH is a full half-circle, from that of the lone outsider yearning for a place within a populated shelter to that of the ruler of the population within the shelter. When Conrad began writing he was identifying himself with a job-applicant, and by the time he wrote his tenth story he was identifying himself with the owner of the company. He had finally arrived at the management point of view.

Marlowe, as narrator as well as central character of the story YOUTH, is Conrad's alter-ego. He recounts his experiences as second mate of a ship bound from London to Bangkok with a cargo of coal, and the vicissitudes of the voyage are the throes of Marlowe's final struggle from boyhood into manhood, his last wrench into maturity. During that voyage Marlowe passed over the line that divides the boy from the man.

The first mishap occurs while the ship is sailing up the English Channel empty, on its way to get the cargo of coal. It is struck a glancing blow by another ship and damaged so severely that the repairs take a month to complete. After then loading the ship and starting their journey to the East, they find that the ship still leaks, and are compelled to put back into port for additional repairs. They set out a second time, only to learn once again that the ship leaks. This time they return to their loading dock, remove the cargo of coal, repair the entire hull, and reload the cargo. The third time that they put out to sea they find their ship seaworthy, the weather favorable, and the crew willing and eager to get on with the trip.

When they are within two hundred miles of Java, however, their cargo of coal catches fire and all hands spend day and night pumping water in and out of the coal bins. Disaster finally overtakes them when an explosion of coal-gas rips great holes in the deck and the fire becomes uncontrollable. A passing ship tows them for a time but soon advises them to abandon the doomed ship. The captain and his crew, instead of boarding the other ship, take to the lifeboats and wait to see their own ship sink. After fitting the lifeboats with some improvised sails, they set out for Java.

Marlowe is in charge of one of the three boats and this is his first command. At the end of several days' rowing and sailing, they reach the Asiatic mainland, with Marlowe in the lead. Everyone is utterly exhausted but also filled with a sense of achievement. This is especially true of Marlowe, who is now at the age of twenty seeing Asia for the first time. The arduous and tragic, but successfully completed, journey had made a man of him. He had met and honorably dealt with the many obstacles which an adverse fortune had opposed to his personal passage from London to Bangkok. He had played a man's part in helping to bring, if not the ship itself, at least the entire crew, without the loss of a single sailor, to its objective on the mainland of Asia. The indomitable future-looking demand of Marlowe the boy to achieve adulthood has reached satisfaction, and in the relating of that success Conrad in effect summarizes his own struggle to reach a point above the melee from which he can look back and down at the partial solutions he had found for his besetting problem.

Chapter 11.

HEART OF DARKNESS

WITH HEART OF DARKNESS (1899) Conrad's art takes a great leap upward to a higher level of performance and meaning, a plateau whereon his theme broadens its range, debates larger issues, and in fact gives body to that maturity which the story YOUTH had merely announced. The outcast-character now no longer sues for admittance into society; it has grown in stature, taken on an air of authority which proceeds from an inner source of strength, and instead of submitting to or seceding from group surveillance it now acts as though it conceives itself to be an independent power capable of weighing the pros and cons of extending diplomatic recognition to the group.

The problems with which the characters struggle in the stories previous to HEART OF DARKNESS would be problems only to child-minds, when compared to those which engage the capacities of Kurtz and Marlowe in Conrad's eleventh story. One has only to imagine Kurtz in Almayer's situation, for instance, to recognize what short work Kurtz would have made of Almayer's problems. Conversely, no Conrad character previous to Kurtz could have even conceived of the problem that killed Kurtz and maimed Marlowe. It is not that Conrad introduces a new problem with HEART OF DARKNESS; it is in essence the same one as he presented in the first ten stories, but it compares to the first ten embodiments of it as does a flower in full bloom to the buds which precede it. With HEART OF DARKNESS Conrad arrived for the first time at a full-dress statement of the knot which he spent a lifetime trying to untie. Kurtz, who killed himself trying to untie it, is the man Conrad might have been, while Marlowe, who lost most of his certitudes in contemplating Kurtz's fate, is the man Conrad became. Kurtz is Conrad's nightmare.

Marlowe, Conrad's alter-ego in this tale, narrates in the first person his experiences during his first and only journey into the African continent. This trip fulfilled his boyhood dream of travelling to the center of Africa, but it also replaced that dream with a nightmare from which he never wholly recovered. His African experience revealed certain things about himself which he would have preferred not to have learned, and he was so maimed by his revulsion against the savage life he found there that he hardly ever felt at home in civilized societies thereafter. He fell in love with savagery but remained defeated and stricken by reason of his inability to embrace and accept the object of his love.

Marlowe's desire to see the interior of Africa is so strong that he resigns his captaincy of an ocean-going freighter in order to make himself available for the first opportunity to become captain of a river steamer in Africa. After much effort and waiting and after a wealthy aunt has interceded for him with the officers of an European firm engaged in the African trade, he secures the employment he desires. The river steamer he is to take charge of travels between two stations on the Congo, both of which are far from the mouth of the river. This necessitates passage as an idle voyager from Europe to the mouth of the Congo and up the river some distance, thence as a marcher in a caravan journey of two hundred miles across a long bend in the river to the Central Station where his boat is located.

While the transport is sailing along the African coast before reaching the mouth of the river, he sees a French gunboat firing shells into an apparently uninhabited stretch of the African continental coastline. At the first trading post thirty miles up the river he sees a chain gang, consisting of six black savages fastened together by chains attached to iron neck-collars. He also sees a large crowd of dying natives lying in a grove, worn out by their work on the railroad which they had been helping to build. One white man too is lying on his deathbed in this trading post; he had been a trading agent in the interior, an employee of the same Company for which Marlowe works.

After a hard, cross-country, fifteen-day march with the caravan, Marlowe arrives at the bend in the river where the Central Station is located—only to find that his ship had been sunk to the bottom of the river by an amateur skipper. It takes Marlowe three months to get the ship raised out of the river bed and back into commission. The monotony of this work, full of frustration, is broken into once by the passage through the post of a trading caravan, on its way to the interior, loaded with worthless trinkets to be traded off to the natives for priceless ivory.

During these three months Marlowe hears a great deal about Kurtz, the manager of the Interior Station. It will be Marlowe's job to transport supplies and merchandise to and fro between the Central and the Interior Stations, and it therefore behooves him to learn all he can about the managers of both Stations. Marlowe becomes greatly interested in Kurtz when he learns that there is a considerable discrepancy between the sentiments about Kurtz publicly expressed by the other employees of the company and their secret feelings about him. The manager of the Central Station tells Marlowe that Kurtz is an extremely good agent and deserves to get a high post in the Administration of the company. However, Marlowe accidentally overhears a conversation in which the same man expresses a hope that Kurtz will die of the fever so that he will never become superintendent. And the brickmaker, the Central Station manager's personal friend who works with Marlowe in repairing the ship, continually pumps Marlowe in an attempt to learn what he may know regarding the plans of the Home Office for Kurtz.

It does not seem to Marlowe that the motive of these people for wanting Kurtz out of the way is a desire that one of them should obtain the high post to which Kurtz, if he lives, may be appointed; it seems to him, on the other hand, that their hatred of Kurtz wells up from a much deeper source of animosity than mere rivalry for a certain position on the company's payroll. Kurtz conceives of himself as a civilizer instead of as an exploiter of the natives, although he nevertheless succeeds in extracting more ivory from the natives than does any other trader. Kurtz's conception of his role in Africa, his fraternizing with the natives, his contempt for the mere commercial view of the company's function on the continent, seems to reduce all the other employees of the company, in their own minds, to accomplices in the shameful transaction of duping the natives, with colored beads and bits of bright cloth, out of their rich store of invaluable ivory. They are perfectly contented in this complicity, their participation in guilt, until a man like Kurtz comes among them and seems somehow to put them in the wrong. Kurtz's notion that to be an employee of the company in Africa is an opportunity to do good to the natives, to benefit them by associating with them and letting them see what a civilized man is like, is in their eyes an affront to the basic principle by which the whole business world lives, namely, that to buy as cheaply as possible and sell as dearly as possible is the very definition of sound practice.

Marlowe's ship is at last ready for the journey up the river to the Interior Station. The manager of the Central Station and a large party of armed men accompany Marlowe as passengers on the boat. Their objective is to get Kurtz, who is sick, bring him back to the Central Station and then, perhaps, send him home to Europe for a rest cure. The armed men are brought along because the natives, who worship Kurtz, may put up some resistance to Kurtz's removal.

They steam up the river for two months before approaching Kurtz's Station. When they have about fifty miles yet to go they find a stack of wood on the river bank with a note pinned on it saying "approach cautiously." When they are anchored because of deep fog about eight miles below the Station, they hear hordes of savages yelling and howling, in sorrowful accents. When they reach the last mile of their journey, they are bombarded with arrows shot at them by the savages hidden in the trees along the banks. The African pilot falls down with an arrow in his side. The armed party on the boat begins firing into the bush with rifles, but all shooting ceases on both sides when Marlowe pulls the steamboat whistle.

They are met at the Station landing by a young Russian, an independent trader and a worshipper of Kurtz. He tells them that the natives had meant no harm by their attack on the boat: they simply did not want anybody to come and take Kurtz away. While the manager of the Central Station and his party, armed to the teeth, go to Kurtz's shed, Marlowe and the young Russian talk. Marlowe learns that the natives worship Kurtz like a god, that Kurtz wanders sometimes alone with a gun and sometimes at the head of an armed party of savages, demands ivory and gets it (the supply of beads and trinkets having been exhausted months ago), that Kurtz takes part in savage religious ceremonies. Marlowe can see a string of fence posts around Kurtz's shed each bearing the head of a decapitated African. The young Russian explains that they are the heads of rebels.

Presently the manager and his armed men emerge from the shed carrying Kurtz on a stretcher; whereupon great numbers of natives move out of the forest from all sides into the clearing and block the way to the boat. They are armed with spears and it is apparent at a glance that the little group of whites could be overpowered in a moment. Kurtz, however, speaks to the assembled natives in tones of command, and the army of black warriors withdraws into the forest. After Kurtz and all the whites are on board ship, however, a savage and superb woman leads the hordes back into the clearing and to the banks of the river. The barbarous and handsome woman stretches her arms out towards Kurtz and makes imploring sounds as though she were wailing in sorrow.

Late that night, Marlowe looks into Kurtz's cabin and finds it empty. He is frightened, because he knows that the number of armed savages assembled at the Station is far more than sufficient to overcome and massacre all the whites on the boat. He is not certain that Kurtz will not order the savages to assault the boat; he has learned from the young Russian that Kurtz himself had ordered the attack to be made on the steamer on its upward journey. Kurtz was of two minds, whether to go back with the steamer or to stay with the savages. Marlowe feels that only he can persuade Kurtz to return to the boat, so he warns no one of Kurtz's escape. He sets out after him, alone and unarmed.

Marlowe finds Kurtz crawling on his hands and knees towards a savage and turbulent ceremonial gathering. The spiritual contest which takes place at this point between Marlowe and Kurtz is the heart of HEART OF DARK-NESS. Marlowe wrestles with Kurtz like Jacob wrestled with the Angel. The most telling argument he uses on Kurtz is the simple statement that if he goes on to join the savages he is "lost—utterly lost." Kurtz's answer whimpers that he was "on the threshold of great things." Kurtz is torn between two great losses.

If he goes back to the savages he will be cut off forever from his civilized European connections, for the manager of

the Central Station is ready to denounce him to the Home
Office for having used guns and violence to extort ivory from
the natives. He will be accepting once and for all time the
ascendancy in his own nature of elements which enslave
him: the impulse to despotic life-and-death power over an
empire of black African savages, the impulse to bask and loll
in the abject worship accorded him as a god by the super-
stitious savages, the impulse to possess the superb and barbarous savage queen who adores him. This is what his great
pretensions to civilize the natives has dwindled into: self-
exaltation. The natives have suborned him by their adula-
tion.

If he consents to go back to Europe, Kurtz will be condemned to marry his "intended," a cultivated woman in a
"Capital City," to compete in a distasteful struggle with
petty commercial minds like that of the manager of the Central Station, and above all to explain why the African chiefs
in the Interior territory have closed the area to all employees of the company except himself.

This dilemma destroys Kurtz, who dies in the boat on
the way back to the Central Station. His last words, as he
contemplates his life with the savages, are "The horror—
the horror." This, however, is not exactly a recantation. It
expresses not only his disgust with what he had discovered
about himself, his desire to be a deity, but also his powerless-
ness before the intensity of this pleasure. It expresses the
intensity of his happiness in Africa.

Marlowe now falls ill and is shipped home to Europe,
taking with him all of Kurtz's private papers. In a way,
Kurtz is Marlowe's alter-ego, and Marlowe goes on living the
life that Kurtz had dropped. He goes back to Europe to
watch, and resent, "the sight of people hurrying through the
streets to filch a little money from each other . . . whose
knowledge of life was to me an irritating pretence, because
I felt so sure they could not possibly know the things I

knew." He had been sick, but "it wasn't his strength that wanted nursing, it was his imagination that wanted soothing." Various people called on him, asking for Kurtz's private papers. An attorney of the company threatened to sue him to get the papers Marlowe refused to relinquish; a journalist acquaintance of Kurtz asked for something; and a man purporting to be Kurtz's cousin wanted to be told about Kurtz's life in Africa and to be given some memento. All of them seemed to Marlowe to be mere scavenging phantoms. He called on Kurtz's "intended" and gave her a bundle of letters. She seemed so unreal too, and her sorrow so irrelevant, that Marlowe had no compunction about telling her a lie: that the last word Kurtz pronounced in life was her name.

All the concerns of men in Europe seemed to Marlowe to be petty and niggardly, of no account, after he had witnessed the denouement of Kurtz's great struggle with the masses of black men in Africa. Kurtz had failed—his only victory had been in that he had retained enough presence of mind to name what he had found in himself there "the horror—the horror." But that failure had been a greater success than any that Marlowe could conceive of any one's having in Europe. Why did not Marlowe go back to Africa and take up Kurtz's life there as Stanley had taken up Livingston's? The answer is simply that he knew he wasn't man enough. It was his pusillanimity that had motivated his successful struggle to rescue Kurtz from throwing in his lot with the savages.

However, Marlowe knew where his heart was, even if his bodily courage was not stout enough to follow it. He had seen a god in action, and he had heard his voice. Kurtz had had a voice like a god's and its tones were to remain louder in Marlowe's ears than anything that was to sound in them thereafter. And behind Kurtz's voice, for Marlowe, is the voice of those millions of irrational savages, all that life which will continue on whether or not Marlowe goes back to watch it. The savages partake of Kurtz's greatness, because they were able, willing, and eager to recognize it and to do obeisance where obeisance was due; while the white employees of the company are base and contemptible jackals, mere ivory-snatchers for the Home Office.

What we have here is obviously a rejection of two groups by Kurtz, and a lukewarm, mitigated, acceptance of one group by Marlowe. However, it is not a deficiency but rather an excess in group-feeling that brings about these total and partial rejections. Both Kurtz and Marlowe are drawn to two incompatible groups, and the savage group is fundamentally incompatible to both men because it is, culturally, so many centuries far back in past time that to commingle with it made Kurtz feel as though his very soul were decomposing within him. Kurtz could not go back that far, and Marlowe much less; but the attempt to do so on Kurtz's part, and the temptation to do so on Marlowe's, destroyed Kurtz's and nearly destroyed Marlowe's ability and desire to regain a place in their natal group. Kurtz strayed so far from his natal group that he could not get back to it, and Marlowe's distance from his group became so great that its gravitational pull on him became faint almost to extinction. The indirectly expressed assumption of the two men's experience is simply that, no matter how disillusioned the individual has become with the motivating values subscribed to by his group, he dies if he permits himself to become totally separated from that group. Both Kurtz and Marlowe sat in judgment on the society from which they sprang, but Kurtz died because he condemned and rejected that society while Marlowe lived because the loss of his esteem for his group did not prevent him from working out a modus vivendi that kept open at least some of the channels of communication between himself and the group to which he belonged.

Chapter 12.

LORD JIM

AFTER THE completion of HEART OF DARKNESS, Conrad returned to the Malay Archipelago for the locale of his next story (LORD JIM, 1900), and he also reverted to the thematic substance of his first story of Malayland, AL-MAYER'S FOLLY. Both Lord Jim and Almayer are anxiety-ridden to a neurotic degree by what they feel to be an unjust and intolerant accusation levelled at them by society. The lives of both men are dominated by the deep resentment they feel against the social group of which they are more or less outcast members, and as a consequence the strongest influence shaping their conduct is their awareness of society's condemnation, overt in Lord Jim's case and covert in Almayer's. Both men are preoccupied with their own mental and emotional reactions to society's opinion of them, in Almayer's case to the opinion he imagines society would have of him were he to return to his native Holland and in Lord Jim's case to the verdict of an Official Court of Inquiry on his conduct as chief mate of the ship _Patna._ Almayer and Lord Jim have each committed an act that has aroused social hostility against them and each has become not only touchy and over-sensitive to the slightest manifestations of this hostility but also over-desirous of vindicating himself in society's eyes and thus regaining some measure of social approval.

Jim had been a parson's son in England and had spent as a boy two years in a training school for ship's officers. While yet a young man, he secured a position in an Oriental

port as chief mate on the *Patna,* an Eastern tramp steamer
bound for the Red Sea with eight hundred Moslem Arab
passengers on a pilgrimage to the Holy Lands.

Several days after leaving port, the ship bumps some
submerged object, probably a sunken ship floating just
beneath the surface, and shortly thereafter the forepart of
the hold is discovered to be full of water and the thin col-
lision-bulkhead amidship to be bulging and throbbing from
the pressure of the water on the other side. The *Patna* is
tilted head down, rear in the air, the entire ship poised
as for a dive to the bottom of the ocean. The chief engineer asserts that the bulkhead will give way at any moment
and sink the ship.

Since this disaster has overtaken them in the middle of
a dark night, since there is apparently no time left in which
to wake the pilgrims and launch them in the lifeboats, since
there would be room in all the lifeboats for less than half
the passengers, and since the captain and all of the officers
except Jim are mere peculators and riff-raff of the Eastern
Ocean, they instantly make haste to flee the ship without
sounding an alarm. Jim refuses to help them launch their
boat, but after they have succeeded without his help and
are calling for the last one of their group, the third engineer, to hurry and jump in before they cast off, Jim, seeing
that the laggard has fallen dead of a heart attack, jumps in
his place. A passing steamer picks up the lifeboat and its
passengers the next morning.

When the steamer reaches its destination, Jim and the
other officers learn, to their consternation, that the ship
Patna had not sunk after all, but had been discovered by
another steamer and towed into port. All the officers
except Jim abscond, but Jim stays to face the Official Inquiry. Marlowe attends the Inquiry as a spectator, curious
to learn what defense can be put up by any ship's officer
who has broken such an immemorial tradition as the one

which forbids an officer to leave a sinking ship unless all of the passengers have first been safely removed. He sees that Jim is, to all appearances, a sound and stalwart English boy of good family and upbringing, and he wants to puzzle out the exact grounds which such a boy as Jim could find for self-justification. Somewhere and somehow a moral cog must have slipped in the boy's mind, and Marlowe wants to see for himself how that slippage could have occurred.

At the Inquiry before the judges and audience, and afterwards in Marlowe's rooms at the hotel, Jim's only excuse is simply that the pilgrims were already as good as dead when he jumped into the waiting lifeboat. If he had waited a minute or two for the ship to start plunging and had then saved himself by clinging to some floating object, he would have incurred no disgrace; so he cannot see how a mere matter of time, such a few moments of time, could make all the difference between disgrace and honor. Some miracle had saved the ship and the lives of the passengers. That miracle had occurred after the ship had been given up as doomed, and therefore could have nothing to do with his personal moral status. Jim insists that he had preserved his honor by ascertaining beyond the shadow of a doubt, before he jumped, that the ship would immediately sink. His only regret now is that he has missed his chance to become a hero. If he had had one doubt that the ship would sink, if he had thought that the ship had one chance in a million of staying afloat, he would have stayed by her—and the miracle of her survival would have made him a hero of the high seas instead of the branded coward he has now become. The Inquiry judges strip him of his Officer's Certificate and he stands stigmatized in the eyes of the public as a deserter from his ship in time of peril.

Marlowe finally sees how the self-deluding process had taken place in Jim's mind. A few instants before Jim jumped, he had seen in his mind's eye, with an intensity of

imagination, all the helpless pilgrims struggling horribly
in the water, engulfed by sudden death. The vividness of
that conjured up scene had been, and was even now, a more
real event to him than the actuality of the pilgrims' safe arrival on shore. His imagined scene was the real thing to
Jim, and the actual occurrence was a miracle, a sort of legal
fiction. It was as though the external world had played a
trick on him, rushing towards him with this cataclysm and
then, when he shut his eyes to receive the blow, veering off
unaccountably in another direction. He felt himself to be
victimized by a sportive and wanton world which did not
fulfill its unalterably announced intentions. The subtle un-
soundness of the man derived therefore from a surplus of
imagination rather than form a deficiency of moral fibre.

Jim's insistence on facing the Inquiry and his belief that
he had not broken the tradition in spite of all the appearances to the contrary convince Marlowe that Jim deserves
some assistance in his fight against universal condemnation.
Jim's imagination may have ambushed his morality, but in
Marlowe's opinion Jim is not a lost man until he condemns
himself. He therefore gives Jim a letter of recommendation,
addressed to an employer of men in another Eastern port,
in which he takes it upon himself to vouch for Jim's good
character. Jim's belief, based on Marlowe's letter, that at
least one man on earth trusts him encourages him to start
a new life and look for one more chance to become a hero.

Jim succeeds in this job and pleases his employer very
much, but when one of the *Patna* officers happens to
find employment in the neighborhood and begins to make
sotto voce allusions to their complicity in disgrace, Jim
throws up his job and disappears. He finds another good job
several hundred miles distant, succeeds in it, and finally
throws it up too when it becomes known that he is one of
the infamous *Patna* officers. This happens again and
again, until Marlowe, who has been following Jim's life

from a distance, decides that he must take a hand in it again.

He tells the story of Jim's life to his friend Stein, a man who owns many trading posts in the Malay Archipelago. Stein diagnoses Jim's case an an instance of the romantic malady, a quixotic and determined endeavor to force the world of his imagination to function within the framework of the actual world of hard realities, and he suggests that the only possible solution for Jim is to immerse himself in a completely secluded segment of the world the hard realities of which could, possibly, be metamorphosed by Jim's personal prowess and creative imagination. Stein knows of just such a little world, a native Malay island on which he owns an unprofitable and practically defunct trading post. The only white man on the island, Stein's employee, has not been strong enough to prevent the natives from splitting into three warring factions; business has therefore been at a standstill for several years. No ship ever stops there except Stein's, and his stops only once a year; the island is consequently a separate little world entirely outside the context in which Jim's past life was located.

Stein had once been a close friend of Doramin, the ruler of one of the three warring groups on the island. When he takes from his finger a ring which had been given him by Doramin and offers it to Jim as a talisman which will give him entree into Doramin's household and, in Doramin's estimation, all of Stein's support, Jim eagerly accepts it. He goes to the island of Patusan as though to a new life on a new earth, not in dejection and defeat but with zeal to embody in his life there those virtues that the Inquiry judges had accused him of not possessing. He feels that, due to the intrusion of a miracle, the old world can never see him as he really is, and that life among the Malays of Patusan will furnish him another opportunity to act out his true self so that it will be apparent to all. He does not think it likely that another miracle will happen.

Immediately upon his arrival in Patusan, Jim is made prisoner by one of the tribes hostile to Doramin. He soon contrives an escape, however, and makes his way to Doramin's stockade. There he is welcomed as soon as he presents Stein's ring, and Dain Waris, Doramin's son, takes an immediate liking to Jim. The two young men become fast friends. Jim persuades first Dain and then Doramin to undertake an attack on one of the rival strongholds, and the strategy which Jim devises turns out to be so successful that the other hostile tribe capitulates without a fight. Within a few weeks Jim has become a legendary figure throughout the island and the real ruler of the entire native population. When Marlowe pays him a visit on Patusan two years later, Jim tells his old friend that all the natives on the island trust him with their lives and that he has established absolute peace between all the warring bands. The natives trust his wisdom and rectitude so implicitly that they ask him to judge disputes between even husbands and wives. Jim has almost forgotten that in the outside world, because of his *Patna* jump, he is considered to be an untrustworthy person. He tells Marlowe that he must hold fast to the natives' belief in him in order to keep in spiritual touch with the people in the outside world, whom he will never see again.

Jim also has a wife. She is Jewel, whose grandfather had been a white man and whose mother, now dead, had been married to Cornelius, manager of Stein's trading post, after her first husband, Jewel's Malay father, had deserted her. Cornelius, a half-mad old derelict, hates Jim for having supplanted him as Stein's representative on the island and for having taken Jewel, his step-daughter and housekeeper, away from him.

Some months after Marlowe's visit to Jim on the island where he is known as the "white king" and "Lord Jim," an unprecedented event takes place. A foraging party of white men, perhaps a dozen in number, invade the settlement. They had come up the forty-mile stretch of river from the coast by longboat after having anchored their schooner on the coast. Their leader is a piratical desperado named Brown. He and his men had stolen the schooner and were in want of supplies to help them on their way to Madagascar, where they plan to sell the ship. It is their intention to pillage and loot the settlement at Patusan in order to obtain the supplies they need.

Jim is absent in the interior when the Brown party arrives. The Malays fire on the longboat and chase its occupants to the top of a hill near the river. There Brown and his men build a barricade around themselves and await developments. Cornelius visits them after dark and tells them about Jim. He strongly urges Brown to kill Jim on sight, asserting that this would so completely cow the natives that Brown and his men could immediately take possession of the whole island. Cornelius brings the men food and water.

When Jim returns from the interior, Dain Waris and Jewel urge him to exterminate the nest of pirates without parley. Jim, however, wants to see for himself whether or not the men are as bad as the Malays suppose them to be. Jim and Brown meet and talk.

Brown does not have the schooner full of armed men that he had pretended to have in his conversations with Cornelius. He therefore had not intended to carry out Cornelius's suggestion that he kill Jim on sight. He had decided to propose to Jim that they join forces, ransack the island, share the spoils and the schooner. But when he sees Jim face to face, he understands at once that Jim is not the kind of man to whom such a proposal can be made. He merely asks for permission to depart in peace and return unmolested to his ship.

Since there has been bloodshed on both sides, the Malays are demanding of Jim that he permit them to exterminate

the marauders. It will not be easy for him to persuade the
natives to grant the strangers safe passage down the river.
He hesitates, ruminating.

Brown then pleads for his life and the lives of his men.
He points out that the numerical odds are two hundred to
one against him and on that basis appeals to Jim's sense
of fair play, asking to be allowed to depart without a fight.
Brown talks on, feeling for a soft spot in Jim. One lucky
stroke was his answer to Jim's question as to what Brown
had done out there, in the outer world, to have become
such an outcast: "I am here because I was afraid once in
my life." Another one was the remark he made in condona-
tion of his having shot and killed one of Dain Waris's men:—
"When it came to saving one's life in the dark, one didn't
care who else went, three, thirty, or three hundred people."
He went on to ask Jim whether "he had nothing fishy to
remember in his own life." Jim's slight but perceptible
responses to those remarks lead Brown on to couple himself
and Jim as sharing a common guilt in being outcasts from
their own people.

And now the miracle takes place a second time. Jim faces
Brown but his eyes examine the ground between himself and
Brown. Brown's eyes, on the other hand, study Jim's face.
While Brown is making an intense effort to understand the
realities of Jim's character, Jim is letting his imagination
construct a fictitious and unreal Brown, a Brown based not
on the realities of Brown's face but upon his false words
and the events in his own past life which they recall. Brown
is in fact gratuitous and unalloyed evil. Jim, however, when
his imagination breaks loose from its moorings, cannot distinguish good from evil. It has broken loose from its moorings now just as it had when he had envisioned the im-
minent sinking of the *Patna*.

Jim begins to conceive of Brown as unfortunate rather
than as evil, as a man who has become evil by force of

circumstances rather than by any intrinsic bent of character. He knows from his own experience how difficult it is for an originally good man not to become evil as a result of his having been accidentally placed in a false position which makes him appear evil. He began to excuse Brown, just as he had excused himself for having made the fatal jump from the *Patna*. At the end of the interview, ⟨Jim agrees to furnish Brown and his men safe conduct back to their schooner.⟩

This second compromise with evil brings about Jim's final undoing. Cornelius guides the pirates' longboat down the river and on the way he shows Brown how to get revenge on Jim and pay him out for having been too good to join forces with him against the Malays. Dain and a group of armed men are stationed along the river near the coast. They have been instructed to allow the Brown party to go unmolested past them towards the schooner. Cornelius, however, pilots the boat into a creek which cuts behind Dain and his men. This gives Brown an opportunity to massacre the Malay band without reprisal. Dain and most of his men are murdered.

Since Jim had given Doramin and the Malay chieftains his guarantee that no harm would come to them from his decision to release the evil white men, he can now no longer command the confidence of the natives. Dain's death at the hands of Brown, whom Jim had vouched for, destroys at one stroke the entire life that Jim had built up around himself on the island of Patusan. He knows that no native will ever trust him again. And since he is directly responsible for Dain's death, he must deliver his own life, in accordance with Malay law, to Doramin, Dain's father. His wife Jewel, and his personal servant Tamb' Itam, urge him to flee from the island. But Jim's decision this time is the right one: he condemns himself. He delivers himself to Doramin, and Doramin shoots him through the heart.

Brown's violation of his safe-conduct privilege and the
safe arrival of the *Patna* in port are equivalent events in
Jim's life. Jim's mistaken clemency in the one case and his
fatal decision to jump in the other, his two great errors
of judgment, spring from one source in his nature: his inability in a time of crisis to hold his imagination in leash.
The story of Lord Jim is not the story of a man who lost
his honor and who tries to win it back; it is the story of a
man whose imagination, instead of throwing light upon and
illuminating the real world, distorts it and betrays him into
unrealistic behavior. LORD JIM is a tragedy of the un-
disciplined imagination and of the untrustworthiness it can
generate even in a man for whom trustworthiness is the most
priceless possession.

The conscientious and sustained effort made by Jim to
prove the judges of the Official Inquiry wrong about him
had ended in failure, and in consequence Jim had rendered
the same verdict on himself in the second instance as the
judges had in the first, thereby admitting his guilt and acquiescing in society's condemnation. By passing sentence of
death on himself he achieved reconciliation with society,
lifted himself out of the class of unregenerate outcasts and
into the class of those whom society has absolved of all offense.

Only by voluntary death could Jim either regain social
approval or retain self-approval, and since he has arrived
at a position wherein he sees eye-to-eye with society these
two approvals are now identical. Jim was a casualty to his
need for group approval: his need for it was so deep that he
was willing to sacrifice his life to obtain it. Almayer took
to opium and dissipation when he lost what he thought was
his last chance to regain social acceptance. Kurtz gave up
the struggle and died when he perceived that to choose membership in either one of the two groups available to him was
irrevocably to lose membership in the other. All three men

met death in their pursuit of public approval and of these three Kurtz endured the greatest suffering in that he had perforce to compel himself to relinquish a public approval that was very dear to him while Almayer and Jim had somewhat inadvertently mislaid theirs by an act committed almost as it were in a moment of absent-mindedness.

Chapter 13.

TYPHOON

IN CONRAD'S next story, TYPHOON (1901), a man's power to solve a difficult problem is presented as a resultant of his deficiency of imagination, the very quality that Lord Jim possessed to such an excessive degree that it tripped him into disaster. Captain MacWhirr is as remarkable for his stubbornly inert imagination as Lord Jim was for the very opposite: his over-active and free-floating imagination. In both stories imagination is a liability: Captain MacWhirr's subnormal imagination enables him to retain his presence of mind when all around him are losing theirs, and Lord Jim's abnormal imagination catapulted him into acts which defeated his deepest purposes.

The role of the imagination in these two stories is not, however, the primary area of concern with which both stories deal. Their common element, and the crux of the matter, is the problem of social cohesion. It is Jim's fate to be repeatedly flung off from, ejected by, the group he belongs to: his problem has to do with a failure of cohesion between himself and his group. In TYPHOON Captain MacWhirr's problem has to do with a cataclysmic debacle of cohesion between all the members of a group of Chinamen who are passengers on his ship. This group has been shattered to atoms, exploded into two hundred mutually repellant particles, dissocialized to the extreme degree that each individual is at war with every other individual in the group. This of course is an intolerable state of affairs and Captain

MacWhirr sedately proceeds to find a way to re-form these two hundred battling Chinamen into a socially harmonious and peaceful group of people. The character of MacWhirr seems to have been intentionally designed by Conrad to form a contrast to that of Lord Jim's, and the contrast is further enforced by the success which attends MacWhirr, the man of common sense and simple probity, in his solution of much the same sort of problem as the one which Lord Jim, the mercurial one, failed to solve.

The situation which confronts Captain MacWhirr and his crew had been created by the typhoon which had tossed the ship so horribly that the passengers' baggage had been shattered and its contents scattered all over the floor of the hold. The two hundred passengers were Chinese coolies on their way home from some construction camp; their baggage consisted of little wooden boxes filled with silver dollars and varying in size because some contained one year's earnings, many two, and a few perhaps five. All the coolies, before the storm, had been huddled in the hold of the ship, each clutching his box; but during the storm every box had been torn out of its owner's arms by the tossing of the ship and broken to pieces. At the height of the typhoon the two hundred Chinese were discovered to be fighting fiercely among themselves for the possession of the silver dollars which, along with the Chinamen, were rolling loose all over the floor.

Commanded to do so by Captain MacWhirr, the crew had stopped the fighting by stringing ropes criss-cross throughout the hold and imprisoning the coolies thereby in long seated rows. The silver dollars had been scooped up in shovels, piled in an empty coalbin, and locked behind its iron doors.

During the remainder of the trip, while the ship steadily approaches its destination at Foochow, the Chinamen are kept locked in the hold. The unanimous opinion of the

crew is that the coolies would, if given the slightest opportunity, attack and murder everybody on the ship, break into
the coal-bin and resume their fierce battle over the silver
dollars. Captain MacWhirr does not divulge his plan for
dealing with the situation which will be facing them after
the ship has reached the dock and the time has come to discharge their passengers, but the crew assumes that he will
summon the Chinese police and relinquish directly to them
the custody of the coolies and their dollars.

The consternation with which the men receive his orders
is therefore unbounded when, upon reaching Foochow, Captain MacWhirr decrees that the Chinamen are to be freed
from the hold and assembled on the deck of the ship. Although nearly overcome with terror, the crew carries out
the order. Through an interpreter the coolies are informed
that the Captain wishes to speak with them in a body on the
upper deck. They peacefully emerge from the hold and
congregate before a table at which Captain MacWhirr is
seated. On the table are stacked all the silver dollars.

The Chinamen listen attentively and in silence while
the captain makes a speech which the interpreter translates.
They are told that the only way in which they can get their
money back is to consent to an equal division among them
of all the dollars. Some will gain and some will lose, in comparison with their original quantities, but all will lose if
the dollars are turned over to a Chinese court for distribu-
tion among them—because the court officials will be sure
to confiscate the larger part of the total sum.

The coolies all profess themselves satisfied with the proposed arrangement and the dollars are therefore equally
distributed among them. This peaceful outcome to a state
of affairs thought by the crew to be fraught with unpredictable hazards effects a complete reversal in the crew's
opinion of their captain. Much the greater part of this
30,000 word narrative consists of letters written by the sea-

men and conversation among them about the stupidity of
Captain McWhirr. The crucial action itself, which casts a
new and transforming light upon everything which has
been said earlier, takes place in the last 1,000 words of
the story. In this crisis, Captain MacWhirr's tenacious grasp
upon the first principles of simple probity produces a strata-
gem which, by its very evident superiority, confounds those
seamen who had looked down upon the Captain with dis-
dain because he was unimaginative and prosaic.

Chapter 14.

AMY FOSTER

WHEN WE move on from Lord Jim and Captain MacWhirr
to Yanko Gooral (in AMY FOSTER (1901)), we see that
Conrad has once again discovered a man whose trouble is
with the group into which circumstance has cast him. In
this story the situation of the alien attempting to secure
a foothold in a hostile foreign land is stripped down to such
raw and naked, elementary essentials that the events narrated
take on an almost nightmarishly primitive quality, and we
feel that the inhabitants of the English countryside, in their
treatment of the shipwrecked Yanko, prove to be only a
shade more civilized than savage and cannibal Africans
might be in their treatment of some unfortunate white man
who had stumbled into their midst. Yanko is the man who
has become separated from his own group, has lost his way
in the world, is just barely tolerated by the strange group
into which he is flung, and is at last fled from in fear and
left to die alone and untended, fatally ill, helpless and un-
befriended. He is the alien whom society will not assimilate,
the man who, transplanted, withers and dies.

Yanko is a Carpathian mountain peasant, sole survivor
of a shipwreck off the English coast. He had been enticed
by unscrupulous recruiters of an American employment
agency to trade his savings for a steamship ticket to the New
World. Terrified by his first trip by train and boat, by the
storm at sea, by the strange clothing and scared look on
the faces of the people whom he accosts after swimming to

shore, he takes refuge in an empty barn. Everyone takes him for an escaped lunatic, because of his incomprehensible language. Amy Foster, the hired girl of the farmer who owns the barn, takes pity on him and brings him a loaf of bread.

Amy had had very little education and had been very well contented with her life as drudge in the farmhouse where she had been working for four years. Since she was noted for her kindness to all living things, the country people thought it was but natural for her to be the first to befriend the wild looking and strange talking foreigner.

After a short time a neighbor farmer offers Yanko a job as his hired man. He proves to be a good worker, strong and dependable; but everybody except his employer and Amy continue to fear and shun the stranger. One day, however, he saves his employer's granddaughter from drowning and is rewarded with title to a cottage and an acre of land. This gives him some status in the community and the country people speak to him occasionally, although for the most part he remains the hated stranger.

When he proposes marriage to her, Amy sees that he is beautiful and accepts him. She goes to live with him in his cottage and for a time they seem to be happy, although they have no social life and learn to speak very little of each other's language. They had been drawn together by their similar status in the rural society, that of hired man and hired girl, by the common dearth of friendship in their lives, and by Yanko's response to Amy's tenderness. Each saved the other from being a solitary social outcast.

Not long after their child is born, however, their almost racial differences from each other begin to count heavily. When Yanko teaches their young son the strange and, to her, incomprehensible Carpathian language, Amy begins to fear her husband in much the same way as do all the other people in the neighborhood. This sense of estrangement so grows upon her that when Yanko falls ill with fever one night and begins talking wildly and deliriously in his foreign tongue, merely asking for a drink of water, Amy becomes so terrified that she seizes the child and runs off with him through the night to her parents' home. Yanko, left without help, dies before dawn.

Conrad lets his heaviest emphasis fall in this story on the stupid inability of the country populace to accept and welcome the innocent stranger in its midst, its irrational fear, suspicion, and near-hatred of the foreigner because of his foreignness. Amy's partial success, by reason of her humanity, in overcoming this basic but unlovely trait in human nature won Conrad's admiration. Even though her mother-love came into conflict with and triumphed over her sense of kinship with a man of virtually another race, she undeniably possessed a virtue which Conrad represents as superior to the smug clannishness of her countrymen.

Chapter 15.

FALK: A REMINISCENCE

FROM ALMAYER'S FOLLY to AMY FOSTER, Yanko
Gooral stands alone among the many men rejected by society as the only one who is guiltless of any real or fancied
offense against society's codes of approved conduct. Yanko's
sole objectionable feature was his foreignness, and even this
counted against him only when, in moments of stress, he
reverted in speech to his native and mysterious language.
In his own mind Yanko knew himself to be innocent of any
wrong-doing. His wife and neighbors condemned him not
because of any deed of his but merely because his strange-
ness made them apprehensive concerning the incalculable
possibilities of conduct of which his alien nature might be
capable. He was a casualty to the provincialism characteristic
of much group-life, to the prejudice of the homogeneous
group against the outsider, and to that tendency of group
members to close ranks upon the approach of the immigrant.
Group exclusiveness in the abstract is clearly the villain of
this story.

The villain of the following story (FALK: A REMI-
NISCENCE (1901)), however, is Falk's secret fear of what
his fellowmen would think of him should they ever come
to know of a certain deed which he had committed in his
past life. The two stories, AMY FOSTER and FALK: A
REMINISCENCE, possess a basic similarity in that each
deals with an individual who is looked at askance by the
group in the midst of which he lives. Both Yanko and Falk

are in some degree comparable to hunted animals, and could conceivably have become the natural quarry of a lynching party had they lived in a community subject to mass hysteria on occasion.

Falk differs from Yanko, however, in that whereas Yanko was queer because he came from a far country, Falk's eccentricities on the other hand are a product of his uneasiness in being the tormented possessor of a guilty secret about himself. Like Almayer and Lord Jim, Falk stands justified in his own eyes; he is not a penitent, burdened with guilt-feelings and self-censure. He merely fears that the public would not think as well of him as he thinks of himself, should a certain factual event in his past life become publicly known. This fear is brought to the high pitch of crisis by Falk's falling in love and his need to share his secret with the girl he loves before she accepts his proposal of marriage.

Falk's occupation is that of tugboat captain in a port several miles up a river located somewhere in the Dutch East Indies. He is not liked in the community; he is taciturn and unsociable, and he never eats meat. This mystifying peculiarity in a society of meat eaters sets him apart from other people since he offers no satisfactory explanation of this idiosyncrasy. Furthermore, Falk had at one time courted a lady of the port city for a long time and had then abruptly stopped visiting her, without having offered the expected proposal of marriage. This strange behavior deepens the mystery of Falk.

The narrator of the story, a ship captain whose boat is being loaded with freight in the port where Falk owns the only tug, spends much of his time visiting another ship captain, a Captain Hermann, whose boat is also being loaded there. Captain Hermann's family travel with him on his ship and attached to the family is a magnificent girl known to us only as Captain Hermann's niece. Falk also comes often to visit with Captain Hermann but he always leaves upon our narrator's arrival. There is much friendly rivalry between the two ship captains in speedy loading of their respective ships.

Our narrator finishes his loading a few hours in advance of Captain Hermann, but he is astonished the next morning when he sees Falk's tugboat escorting Captain Hermann's ship down the river instead of his own. He rushes off to the charterer's office to enter a complaint and is informed that Falk has refused to take his ship out tomorrow or any other time. No one knows what Falk's motive is for this outrageous behavior. However, the narrator finally learns from Schomberg, the hotel proprietor, that Falk has been courting Captain Hermann's niece and thinks that the narrator has been courting her too. The only other person in the settlement who can pilot a ship down the river is a former ship captain who has gone native. The narrator hunts and finds him, only to learn that Falk has already preceded him and bribed the man not to give him any assistance.

That evening the narrator encounters Falk in the hotel barroom, accosts him and asks for a private interview. Falk consents. After several hours talk, the narrator finally persuades Falk to take his ship down the river by promising to intercede with Captain Hermann for his consent to the marriage between the niece and Falk. Falk tells him that Captain Hermann himself has been speaking of the narrator as a possible suitor for the niece, thus inciting Falk's jealousy.

When they arrive at the mouth of the river where Captain Hermann's ship is anchored, the narrator keeps his bargain. Captain Hermann dislikes Falk, but he consents to abide by his niece's decision, whatever it proves to be. Falk then announces that he has a communication to make to them all. They listen in consternation while he recounts his experience on a disabled ship floating out of the paths of shipping toward the South Pole. When the food ran out, the captain had committed suicide. Soon the entire crew except Falk and the ship's carpenter were too weak to walk. The carpenter tries to kill Falk but is killed by him instead. Falk and the starving crewmen then eat the slain carpenter, and later one by one the weakest sailors are killed and eaten by the remaining stronger ones. Falk alone survives, to be rescued by a whaling ship.

Before he could ask any woman to become his wife, Falk felt compelled to unburden himself of this secret. Justified in his own mind by the fact that death had at the time been his only alternative and that the men he had killed and eaten had been intent on killing and eating him, Falk nevertheless possesses no confidence that the public would accept those grounds as sufficient justification for his having, none the less, killed and eaten his shipmates. He has hope, however, that a prospective wife might find it possible to share his self-sanction.

Captain Hermann was horrified, just as Falk had feared; the niece, however, pities him and agrees to the marriage. Captain Hermann's hysterical outburst of denunciation upon hearing Falk's secret convinces no one. It is recognized by everyone present at Falk's confession as the mere conventional outcry always raised by the weak who fear to be seen condoning on any grounds whatever actions society considers reprehensible. The central issue with which the narrative is concerned is not the morality of Falk's cannibalism but the conflict between Falk's need to confess the dark passage in his life and his fear that his confession will drive away from him the girl he loves.

His treatment of his fancied rival, the narrator, resembles his treatment of his shipmates on the stricken ship, and indicates that his need for the girl is as intense as had been his desire to live when he ate human flesh in order to survive. It is his need for the girl that forces this secret, guarded so carefully all these years, out of him. He had finally bolted from the other girl he had courted, because he could not overcome his extreme reluctance to expose himself to the conventional outcry with which an unfeeling public is wont to pelt the taboo-breaker. But his need to confess, which is almost identical to his need for love, finally overcomes that reluctance. Captain Hermann's vituperation carries off in its flood the final debris and vestiges of Falk's horror of himself. The tirade, in effect, gives Falk a sense of absolution, and he can now marry his girl with a clear conscience.

Chapter 16.

TOMORROW

THE DESIRE to marry is the propelling force in the action not only of FALK: A REMINISCENCE but also of Conrad's next story, TOMORROW (1902). Bessie Carvel, Falk, and Yanko Gooral: all three were lonely persons for whom marriage seemed to represent some measure of rescue from isolation. In fact, lonesomeness itself could be considered as the basic theme of these three stories, since each of the three persons about whom the action of the stories is gathered is conscious of his solitude and somewhat depressed by it. The difference between these three studies of solitude is that while in AMY FOSTER our attention is directed at the cruelty of a group which cold-shoulders a visitor in its midst, and in FALK: A REMINISCENCE at the motivations which cause a man both to inflict solitude on himself and to seek reconciliation with society when solitude becomes intolerable, in TOMORROW it is directed at the ways in which the solitary life promotes disease and distortion in the activities of the imagination. These three stories are about three unhappy people, and Conrad locates the source of their unhappiness in the fact that their lives are virtually devoid of group relationships.

Bessie Carvel, in TOMORROW, permits herself to be cajoled into hoping for an improbable event miraculously to happen, and consequently learns to her sorrow that the road of the unleashed and unrealistic imagination leads not to the anticipated happiness but only to a rude awakening.

Instead of using her imagination as a power with which to penetrate the secret nature of the real world already in existence about and around her, she uses it to dream of an unlikely though possible event which would transform that reality into something new and strange. Through this illegitimate and romantic use of the imagination she comes to grief.

Bessie was not an easy victim, however. The dreary circumstance of her life as nurse to a blind, half-paralyzed and tyrannical father, combined with the charming prospects evoked in her mind by the repeated assertions of the courteous old man next door that his runaway son would soon return home and instantly fall in love with her, would have sorely tested the resistance of a very strong girl indeed. Bessie resisted as well as she could, but by reason of the very dreariness of her life she could not but be amenable to the power of reiterated and romantic suggestion.

Captain Hagberg, the old man next door, had come to live in this English hamlet because he had once received a letter stating that his long-lost son is sometimes seen in the neighborhood. The old demented captain advertises in the papers for his son Harry, and he tells Bessie, the daughter of his next-door neighbor, that Harry will see the advertisement "tomorrow," return home, fall in love with her at first sight and marry her. At first, Bessie merely smiles at the old man's credulity, pleased and flattered at the implied compliment and gratified in spite of herself that anyone should conceive of her as an object of romance. But as time wears on, she secretly begins to hope for Harry's return, and for the miracle of romance to occur between himself and her. She comes to imagine that he is her absent lover, although she admits it not even to herself.

For this sin of her imagination against reality, Bessie was not greatly culpable. The degree of temptation to which she was subjected was magnified by the loneliness of her life with the two old men. She gave way little by little, and pardonably, to the contagious inextinguishability of hope evinced by the half-demented Captain Hagberg, and she herself did not realize how far she had gone until the long lost young man Harry finally does make his appearance.

When Harry knocks at his father's door one evening, Bessie watches him from her window. She sees Captain Hagberg refuse to recognize his son, throw a spade at him and call him an impostor. The old man had expected his son to be a young boy instead of this grown and unrecognizable man: he does not realize how many years have passed since his son ran away. Bessie goes to Harry and tells him about his father, urging him to be patient with the old man. She even tells him that his father has gone so far as to select a girl for him to marry. Harry scoffs at the idea of marrying and settling down in such a tiny hamlet. He says too that his father is the same spade-throwing old man that he had run away from as a boy and that there would be no point in his waiting for a reconciliation. As he shows signs of leaving, Bessie's suppressed and unadmitted love for him springs into immediate vibrant life, and her agitation reveals to Harry that she is the girl whom his father wants him to marry. He expresses some compunction for the ribald freedom with which he had tossed away the suggestion of matrimony, now that he has guessed Bessie's personal involvement in his destiny. However, he does not retract his words; he merely goes on to explain that he is an inveterate rover, not only from town to town but from girl to girl, and therefore cannot be a husband. He borrows money from her, gives her a few passionate kisses, and walks quickly away. She remains still, as if stunned, for a few moments, then rushes into the street and calls his name in a loud, desperate cry. But he is out of sight. Captain Hagberg hears her cry, comes to his door and tells her to forget that "grinning, information fellow," that the true Harry will come "tomorrow."

Bessie's romance, aside from her unacknowledged anticipations, had lasted but a brief half-hour. When Harry walked swiftly away from her, he took with him not only the physical reality of his person but also the imagined reality which had come to fill such a large part of Bessie's conscious life. The loudness of the cry with which she had attempted to call him back to her measured the extent of destruction which Harry's brief appearance and swift departure had effected in the imaginative life of her mind. The severity of her punishment seems excessive, until we reflect that it is no greater than that meted out to all without exception who, instead of utilizing their imagination to illuminate the real and the given, misuse it to create an illusory world of phantasm which one touch of reality can shatter.

Chapter 17.

THE END OF THE TETHER

AFTER COMPLETING the preceding three stories of people who are suffocating for want of active participation in the social life of a group, Conrad turned his attention once again, as in HEART OF DARKNESS, to the obverse of that theme: the dilemma of a man who finds himself torn between his conflicting personal loyalties to two separate groups. THE END OF THE TETHER (1902) and HEART OF DARKNESS are similar in that each deals with a man whose dual membership in groups with opposing interests kills him, and they differ in that Kurtz's death in HEART OF DARKNESS is an absolute loss to both societies while Captain Whalley's in THE END OF THE TETHER enables him to succeed in fulfilling his obligations to both groups. All five of these stories, these two and the three which precede THE END OF THE TETHER, are rooted in the same thematic subsoil, since their basic concern is with a disorder in, a frailty of, or a disability caused by the absence of, the connecting link which joins the individual to the group.

Captain Whalley feels that he owes equal allegiance to two separate loyalties. They had been compatible with each other until circumstances beyond his control rendered them irreconcilable except by that most drastic of all devices: suicide. In order to protect one of the loyalties he had been forced temporarily to jeopardize the other, and during that period of danger an event occurs which will force him to retrieve at once the one which is in jeopardy, to take it out of pawn, as it were. To make this attempt, however, will place both loyalties in even greater jeopardy. Only by suicide can he insure the safety of both.

Two simultaneous misfortunes happen to Captain Whalley and lead to the impasse which gives his courage and fortitude its final test: his fortune, built up by careful saving of his earnings as a ship captain, disappears in the bankruptcy of the firm in which his money is invested, and his son-in-law, the support of Captain Whalley's daughter and grandchildren, dies and leaves his family destitute. The pleasure-yacht that is the sole remnant of Captain Whalley's fortune is sold to buy a boarding house for his daughter and a half-interest in a small freighter to provide income for himself and his daughter's family. The purchase-price of the half-interest is to be refunded to Captain Whalley after three years, during which time he is to function as Captain of the ship in return for one half the profits gained in freighting.

During the three-year period Captain Whalley's eyesight begins to fail. He cannot resign his command because his investment will be forfeited unless he finishes his three-year term as Captain, and he cannot reveal his disability to the owner of the ship, because the owner is so hard-pressed for capital that he would take advantage of this opportunity to confiscate the investment. Captain Whalley solves this problem by hiring a Malay serang to pilot the ship for him. The landmarks are so well known to Whalley that he can guide the ship by proxy, depending entirely on the Malay's answers to his question concerning the position of beacons as they come into view.

The owner of the ship is its chief engineer, Mr. Massy. He needs money so badly for new boilers that he continually presses Whalley to leave his investment in the venture for another three years and even to increase it. Massy's desperation at the near approach of the date upon which he must return Whalley's money to him finally becomes so great that, upon receiving Whalley's final refusal to continue the partnership, he hits upon a frantic expedient as a solution to his difficulties. Near the compass he hangs a coat, the pockets of which are loaded with magnetic iron. The Malay serang consequently changes the course of the ship and during the night it crashes on a rocky reef. Captain Whalley accidentally finds the coat while the ship is sinking, accuses Massy of the crime and savagely threatens to expose him to the Court of Inquiry. Massy replies that if he does, the insurance money will not be paid and Whalley will lose his investment.

Captain Whalley realizes that in a few weeks he will be totally blind and that the sinking of the ship will be attributed to his blindness, that his tale about the coat-load of magnetic iron will be discredited. In either case the insurance money will not be paid and his daughter will lose the only capital between herself and destitution. Furthermore, his own honor will be lost when it becomes known that he had, though blind, continued to act as captain of the ship, thereby making it unseaworthy.

The sinking of the ship, with its attendant Inquiry, will discover to the world that he is blind and his disgrace will be published abroad, whether or not the blindness is taken to be the cause of the sinking. He will have failed in responsibility to both his loyalties, one being the obligation to so conduct himself at all times as to maintain the high esteem in which the profession of ship's officer is publicly held, and the other being the obligation to furnish adequate financial support to his widowed daughter and her children.

Should he go down with the ship, however, the insurance money will be paid, the amount of his investment will be placed in his daughter's hands, his blindness will remain an undiscovered secret and his personal honor will avoid public blemish. Only by suicide can Captain Whalley succeed in achieving the objectives for which he has been striving and in eluding the disasters which have been pursuing him. He quickly thinks through his alternatives, and while the crew is clambering down into the lifeboats he makes his decision. When it is his turn, the last, to leave the sinking ship, he is nowhere to be found.

By going down with his ship, Captain Whalley outwitted an adverse fate and overcame the circumstances which were opposing him. His suicide was not a giving up of the fight, a laying down of his weapons, but the final great exertion by which he won the war.

Chapter 18.

NOSTROMO

UPON COMPLETING the story of Captain Whalley, Conrad must have felt that he had now run one full circuit round his basic theme, had entered and studied it from all essential directions and vantage points, because he now embarks upon the greatest creation of his career. His novel NOSTROMO (1904) is the apex of his lifework, the very pinnacle of Conrad's achievement. It compares with his previous pieces of fiction as a circle compares to a series of arcs or as a globe does to a spherical sector. All the partial points of view presented in the stories from THE BLACK MATE to THE END OF THE TETHER are gathered up into one total view in NOSTROMO.

In essence, the novel NOSTROMO is a study in group formation, and its core meaning may be stated as follows: when the process of group formation is fully understood, the fact becomes clear that society and its outcasts are essential to each other. All of Conrad's previous stories, except YOUTH, are written more or less from the point of view of an individual experiencing some sort of trouble in his relation to society; but NOSTROMO is written more closely from the point of view, not only of society itself, but that of the men of power, the "old men of the tribe," the decision-makers for the total community, the authorities who determine the policy of the group. In this novel a nation falls apart, a revolution occurs, a part of the nation secedes and sets itself up as a separate and independent State: a new society is created.

Conrad presents these events in the form of a realistic political history of a fictitious State, rather than in the form of a novel in the usual sense. He does not take us inside the consciousness of any of the characters nor does he tell us anything about what is going on in their minds that cannot be inferred from their external behavior. There is no narrator-participant in the action itself, although the impersonal historian seems to have been an eye-witness to most of the events which he records.

As one society disintegrates and another grows up in its place, persons who were outcasts in the old society become respected citizens in the new, and vice versa, so that the stigma of social disapproval is seen to be a social phenomenon rather than a matter of personal good and evil. And, above all, the material and economic roots for both the cohesive and the ostracizing tendencies in human associations are laid bare. This removes them from the category of acts which involve guilt-feelings and neutralizes the stigma attached to the outcast status. By writing this novel as though he were a socio-political historian describing an actual group-formation taking place on a national scale, Conrad gains a coign of vantage so far "above the melee" that the lofty perspective itself becomes an instrument of understanding and in consequence the social outcast is seen in relation to the total structure of society.

Finally, in making clear by means of this novel the necessary conditions on which the success of a political revolution depends, Conrad is by indirection succeeding in placing on record an impression of the feelings which had dictated his own personal abandonment of his family's participation in the Polish revolutionary struggle against Russia.

The true protagonist in NOSTROMO is really not a person but a force which Conrad calls "material interests."

This force transforms the fictitious Central American province of Sulaco from an agrarian to an industrial society and leads to its secession from its parent State of Costaguana and its establishment as an independent nation. The characters in the narrative are actors in the great drama of revolution and secession, but the greatest actor of all is the "material interest" which uses the action of the characters to gain its own end. Even Charles Gould, the man whose personal initiative first set these material interests in motion, is himself but a puppet through which their power manifests itself.

The history of Costaguana had long consisted of series after series of revolutionary upheavals and civil wars. Abstractions, such as the liberal political ideas of rationalist and humanitarian reformers, had failed to bring peace to Costaguana or freedom from periodic seizures of dictatorial power by rival generals of the Army. The State, theoretically composed of elected representatives voted into office by popular ballot, had been during most of its life the legitimate prey of unscrupulous political or military adventurers.

When Charles Gould had first come to Sulaco to mine the silver buried in the nearby mountains, he had been astute enough to place many of the government officials on his secret payroll in order to protect his enterprise from the disorderly, irresponsible, and immoderate exactions of the taxing authorities. Successive political adventurers who had seized control of the State and its taxing power had levied so many forced loans upon Charles Gould's father that the family fortune had dwindled, by the time it came into Charles' hands, to an old unused silver mine. When his father dies, Charles has just turned of age in England, where he has been at school for over ten years. He marries an English girl, persuades a North American capitalist to finance him, and goes to Sulaco to open the old mine.

The veins of ore prove to be very rich, and the San Tome

Mine soon becomes a great power in Sulaco, protected from the depredations of the corrupt and piratical government by the strategic secret payroll which Gould's agent distributes in the capital city of Costaguana. The dictator at the head of the State was fortunately strong enough to retain his power, suppressing all rival factions, for a period of twelve peaceful years, during which time the San Tome Silver Mine grew unmolested into a great enterprise, employing many men. The National Central Railway, encouraged by Gould's success in the hitherto politically unstable country, begins to build extensive new lines throughout the nation, and the Oceanic Steam Navigation Company, with offices in Sulaco, grows rich on the revenue earned by carrying the San Tome silver to the world's markets. These three big businesses have become a stabilizing factor in the political economy of Costaguana.

Gould's San Tome Mining Company had in fact become so strong a power that when the dictator dies and civil war breaks out among the General-led factions, Gould's financial support of a man whom the more enlightened and liberal civilian families have asked to assume the dictatorship results in quick success, the suppression of the contending and unscrupulous Generals, and the restoration of peace, law, and order. If let alone to make his own decision, Gould would have thrown his support to the strongest personality among the contending Generals, the one most likely to retain his power, by whatever means, the longest. But he had been persuaded by Don Jose Avellanos, a prominent liberal reformer, to support the enlightened and honest but weak Ribiera. Gould's principal motive, aside from his pleasure in doing as his friend Avellanos wishes, is not a humanitarian sympathy with the Costaguana people and a desire to relieve them of their oppressive war-lord dictators but a desire to have a man at the head of the State whose underlings will not have to be bribed and placed on a secret payroll. He hopes that his material interests and Avellanos' abstract philosophic ones will work together for the same end, protection for the San Tome Mine principally, and for the common people incidentally, against the depredations of money-hungry, tax-gathering Generals.

However, Ribiera the liberal failed to consolidate his position and within six months was faced with revolution. He had used Gould's money to equip and arm one of the contending Generals who in return had suppressed the other Generals and supported Ribiera for President. Ribiera had then rewarded this man, General Montero, by making him Minister of War in the new government. All effective military power is therefore in Montero's hands instead of in Ribiera's, and it is not long before General Montero decides that he rather than Ribiera should be President.

Only the capital city itself, which is located inland on the far side of the mountains which separate Sulaco from the rest of Costaguana, and the province of Sulaco remain loyal to Ribiera. All the other provinces respond to Montero's inflamed accusations that the so-called liberal Ribiera had allowed the foreign capitalists to steal the country's wealth from the people. Montero's armies lay siege to the capital city but are held at bay for a time by the National Guard.

Don Jose Avellanos, the man of abstract ideals and liberal views, the philosophic historian of Costaguana, takes charge of the Ribierist campaign to defeat General Montero. He sends money, which Gould supplies, to Paris for guns and ammunition and he persuades a young Costaguanian there, Martin Decoud, to superintend the purchase of war material. Decoud, a young intellectual emigre from Costaguana, has become a Parisian boulevardier, and a contributor of articles about the politics of his native country to Parisian journals.

He accompanies the ship load of ammunition back to Sulaco, mainly because he remembers how lovely Avellanos' daughter Antonia had been as a child when he attended school with her in Paris. A political skeptic, Decoud regards the attempt of Avellanos to set up a stable, liberal, and reformed government in Costaguana as a mere "ploughing of the sea," but he nevertheless upon his arrival in Sulaco allows himself to be persuaded by Avellanos into editing a Ribierist newspaper.

An army is organized in Sulaco with San Tome money and sent across the mountains to relieve Ribiera in the capital. Before it arrives, however, General Montero's troops have overpowered Ribiera's National Guard and captured the city. Ribiera escapes into the mountains and flees toward Sulaco. The most trusted active young man is Nostromo, head-foreman over the longshoremen whose main duty is to warehouse and guard the silver from the mine and load it into the O.S.N. steamships. Nostromo successfully whisks Ribiera away from his pursuers, through a mob of Monterist sympathizers in Sulaco, and on board a waiting steamship.

News comes that two Monterist armies are approaching Sulaco, one by land and one by sea. Their objective is to take possession of the San Tome Mine and to confiscate the warehouses of silver.

Gould sends the ever trustworthy Nostromo to sea in a small lighter loaded with all the silver from the warehouse and instructs him to intercept any northbound ship and ask it to take him and the silver to North America. However, during the night the lighter is accidentally rammed by the Monterist ship entering the harbor. The lighter is partially disabled, but Nostromo succeeds in getting it beached on a small desert island. He unloads the silver, buries it in the side of a hill, and returns to Sulaco, sinking the lighter before he arrives. The Monterist ship-captain had reported crashing a lighter and sinking it; Gould therefore believes that the silver is lost. Nostromo's reappearance is attributed to his swimming prowess. Since Nostromo does not see Gould in person but is immediately sent on another important errand, he does not mention that the silver is safe.

The Monterist generals have demanded from Gould the keys of the mine but have been told that the mine has been loaded with dynamite and that if either Gould or his mine is molested the dynamite will be ignited and the mine destroyed. The generals do not want to be responsible for having brought about the destruction of Costaguana's most valuable property and they therefore mark time while awaiting instructions from Montero himself.

Nostromo's third great assignment is to take a locomotive through the enemy lines to the army which had been sent to relieve Ribiera, request it to return at once and oust the Monterist forces from Sulaco. Gould has decided not only to use his private army, formed by a combination of the government forces in Sulaco with the forces of Hernandez, a bandit with a price on his head, to protect his mine and to defend the city and province of Sulaco from the main Monterist army, but also to use it as a force with which to set up a local secessionist government in Sulaco, independent of Costaguana.

These plans are all accomplished, and thus a new political State is born. Peace and stability come to Sulaco at last —and not from the hands of the enlightened liberals but from the hands of a business man for whom peace and stability are an economic necessity. Material interests impose peace by force on a country which had degenerated from democracy and representative government through demagoguery to a series of corrupt military dictatorships. When it is proposed some years later that Sulaco annex the remainder of Costaguana in order to rescue its people from the oppression of the war-lords, Gould rejects the proposal on the ground that "material interests" do not require such an enterprise.

An epilogue to this history now occurs in connection with Nostromo and the hidden silver. Since everyone assumes that the silver had gone down with the sunken lighter, Nostromo decides not to reveal the truth about it but to "get rich very slowly." The new State has presented him with a small schooner in recognition of his services during the secessionist war. Nostromo sails up and down the coast carrying freight and occasionally selling in distant cities a few bars of silver which he has secretly and after dark removed from its hiding place.

When a lighthouse is built on the desert island, the job of lighthouse keeper is given to the father of Nostromo's intended wife. This enables Nostromo to visit the island openly, but he nevertheless does not visit his cache of silver until after he has made it appear to the girl and her father that he has left the island and gone home for the night. One late evening the father therefore mistakes him for an unauthorized prowler, shoots and kills him.

In this compressed recapitulation of the complicated plot of a very long novel, much has been omitted. The omitted parts, however, merely supplement the chain of events as recounted above. The main line of action sufficiently indicates that Gould rather than Nostromo is the central character of the novel, its subject Gould's political power rather than Nostromo's defalcation, and its theme the economic root of all effective social and political power.

Throughout this entire account of the history of Sulaco, the determinant factors are shown as materialistic rather than ideational. The ideational succeed only when they find themselves fortuitously coinciding with some material interest. When they conflict, material interest wins, as it did in

Nostromo's case when his own material interest in the boat-load of silver clashed with the unmitigated trustworthiness which had been the motif of his life.

This novel was apparently meant by Conrad as a corrective to the unrealistic, intellectualist assumption of nineteenth century political liberalism that ideas alone, unimplemented by the power of economic interest, can affect the course of history. One of the minor but very significant characters, to whom much space is devoted, is Giorgio Viola, an Italian refugee once closely associated with Garibaldi. Viola's conversation is replete with windy abstractions about freedom and liberty. We are led to contrast the ineffectuality of his purely verbal political activity, and that of Avellanos, with the very practical and real power which Gould exercises with few words and much restraint.

Other minor but important characters, important because they are rays of light focussed on the main theme, are Hernandez, Martin Decoud, and Dr. Monygham. Each of these, like Nostromo, are either deviants from one group or another or casualties of the group formation process.

Hernandez, the outlaw with a price on his head (outlawed originally because he had fought on the losing side of a previous revolution) becomes Minister of War in the new State of Sulaco. He is the man to whose lair in the mountains the respectable families of Sulaco fled for protection when General Montero's army was advancing on the city.

Martin Decoud, an intellectual skeptic who feels all group-formation to be a mere "ploughing of the sea" since he himself is devoid of any feelings of attraction to any group, commits suicide when the misfortunes of war sever what tenuous group-ties remain to him after his dissolvent mental analysis of them has done its work. Decoud, like Conrad himself, had left his homeland, abandoning personal participation in the revolutionary struggles for socio-political improvement, and we feel that Decoud represents for Conrad a state of mind he himself would surely have fallen into had he not been able to hammer out for his own use an understanding of the functional relation that subsists between the individual, however nonconformist, and the group.

Dr. Monygham is an unusual and rare variant of the outcast mentality. He is described as a man at whom people "looked askance as a sort of beachcomber of superior intelligence partly reclaimed from his abased state." Having many years ago been forced by a political tyrant to confess under torture to deeds he had never committed and to implicate others who were innocent, Dr. Monygham has ever since been ashamed, as well as embittered and cynical. His rehabilitation and recovery of self-respect comes about through his finding himself able to be of assistance to the Sulaco forces in the secessionist war, and he becomes in time State Inspector of Hospitals, a leader in the group which founds the new nation. The indispensability to each other of the outcast and the social order is the specific meaning embodied in the person of Dr. Monygham, and that Conrad meant him and his function to be integral to this novel is enforced by the fact that he places Dr. Monygham at the center of every crisis in the clash between the Monterist and the secessionist forces. Decoud and Monygham are the two most meaningful characters in the novel, and in their disparate destinies are to be found the hidden core of Conrad's feeling about the necessity of the group-tie for the individual.

The root idea to which this novel gives expression is allied to that which underlies "Lord Jim" and "Tomorrow." These two fictions have to do with the use and misuse of the personal, and "Nostromo" of the political, imagination. Both fail when they become detached from, or succeed when they remain firmly moored to, certain basic realities, realities from which both kinds of imagination are extremely prone to disengage themselves. The political theorist, whether he is attempting to understand and interpret the history of the past or to exert an influence on the history to come, is apt to forget that economic realities count more heavily than all others. So also does the theorist of the personal life, whether in explaining to himself his past actions or in planning a future which he desires to bring to pass, often disable his imagination by allowing it to slip free from the unalterable fact or event which should fetter as well as fertilize it.

Chapter 19.

THE INFORMER

SINCE EXAMINATION of Conrad's first eighteen stories has disclosed Conrad's feelings as converging for focus on the reciprocal and value-creating need subsisting between the individual and the group, it is not surprising to find that he now proceeds to perform an autopsy on a man who pretended to be a member of a group only in order the more effectively to destroy it. The character of the police-spy seems to have had a peculiar fascination for Conrad, because he gave extended and complete treatment to this type of person three separate times in his fiction, and each time a perceptible amount of horror appears as an ingredient in his emotional attitude towards the character. When one considers the supreme value which Conrad placed on the individual-group relation, it seems but natural that perfidiousness in this setting should represent for him the supreme evil.

In each case Conrad gives his attention primarily to the nature of the moral injury inflicted by the police-spy upon himself rather than upon the injury suffered by the group. Conrad apparently grants no concession whatever to the common assumption that a man escapes self-injury if the deception he practices on one group of which he pretends to be a member is meant to further the interest of another group to which he is devoted. Group membership in itself seems to be in Conrad's view of such intrinsic great worth that for any individual to make use of any group acceptance in order

to further an ulterior end hostile to that group is an offense insupportable and therefore disintegrating to that individual.

In THE INFORMER (1905) Comrade Sevrin and Lady Amateur are members of an illegal, anarchist, revolutionary society in London. Sevrin is a police-spy pretending to be a bona fide anarchist, while Lady Amateur is an upper-class socialite dabbling in anarchist activities out of boredom. These two think that they are in love with each other, but during the story each discovers that self-deception had been the penalty each had earned by pretending to be members of a group to which they do not truly belong.

They learn to their great surprise that they have been in love not with each other but with a false mental image which each has created in the other's mind. Both have been tricked by their imagination into believing that the other was in truth what he and she merely appeared to be, and they discover that each has been in love with the appearance rather than with the person. Without realizing it, each had been in love with an idea inside of his and her own head instead of with any external reality. The external reality of each had seemed for a time to correspond exactly with the purely subjective image which subsisted in the other's mind. Since their love was based upon this correspondence instead of upon self-revelation of each to the other, it vanished in an instant when they found each other out.

So far, this analysis of Comrade Sevrin's and Lady Amateur's relation seems to be that of most tentative love affairs and of many marriages. But the difference in this case is that Comrade Sevrin staked his life upon the accuracy of his mental image of Lady Amateur—and lost it. He was, furthermore, a professional disguiser himself and ought therefore to have been even more able than any ordinary man to penetrate a disguise. The meaning of the story resides in its clarification of the process by means of which Comrade Sevrin came to be so completely deceived.

The Chief of the revolutionary group to which Comrade Sevrin and Lady Amateur belong suspects that some one of its members might be a police spy, since the plots hatched by this group have so consistently miscarried, and he therefore decides to stage a fake raid by anarchists from another group disguised as policemen. He hopes that the spy will reveal his identity in some way to the supposed police.

This strategy would have failed to ferret out the impostor, had not Sevrin been terrified that one of the anarchists might, during the fracas, endanger the life of Lady Amateur by throwing a bomb at the raiders. In order to protect her from this not only possible but very real danger, Sevrin reveals his identity to the supposed police and orders them to take the girl to safety before they approach the man who has the bomb. The fake police have not given him an opportunity to speak to them in private, and therefore Sevrin is forced to expose his police affiliations not only to them but also to the assembled anarchists and, above all, to Lady Amateur. In doing so, he risks his life for her sake, because he knows quite well that his fellow members of the anarchist group will have their vengeance on him.

In only one way can he possibly escape that vengeance. If Lady Amateur loves him enough to stand by him, respect and understand him, and respond as a true lover would to the words he now addresses to her—"I have been thwarting, deceiving, and betraying—from conviction. Do you understand what that means? From conviction."—she may be able to save his life. He wants, at the very least, to stand justified in her eyes. He thinks that she loves him' enough to share any announced conviction of his, however inconsistent it might be with her preconceived ideas about him.

This crisis brings each of them face to face with the other's real self for the first time. When Lady Amateur rejects his plea, she in effect declares to herself as well as to him that she had been in love with the anarchist, not the

JOSEPH CONRAD:

man. And Sevrin learns by her action that he had mistaken her gestures of love towards the actor's part he had been playing for the reality of love towards the man he was. What he had taken for love had been mere pantomime, and he had loved, not the real woman who was a pantomimic, but a fictitious woman whom his own imagination had created. They had thought that they loved each other, but they had been wrong: they had merely loved each other's parts in the drama of revolutionary action.

Both had been deceived, but Comrade Sevrin's deception was the deeper. Both had been poseurs, but Lady Amateur had been the unconscious dupe of her own pose and had nothing to offer when the play was over, while Sevrin had torn off his mask, the achievement of a lifetime, in the mistaken belief that Lady Amateur experienced emotionally the feelings which her gestures simulated. She was neither a lover nor an anarchist, but she had succeeded in persuading herself as well as as Sevrin that she was both. Her inability to stand by him in his peril was motivated not by her loyalty to the anarchist group but by her incapacity to love.

The bona fide anarchists had not taken Lady Amateur to be a woman of conviction; they had merely accepted her as a harmless and somewhat helpful addition to their staff. How did Sevrin come to be so greatly deceived in her? Conrad says that since Sevrin was "an actor in desperate earnest himself, he must have believed in the absolute value of conventional signs." But perhaps this is only a clue to Conrad's deeper meaning. Sevrin obviously did not believe in the absolute value of his own "conventional signs. "It will not do merely to say that he has been blinded by love. He was a very able man who had made a serious mistake in judgment. He had lost the power to distinguish the imitation from the real thing, and this loss represents the price he paid for his acquired but consummate ability to impersonate a character whose convictions were the exact opposite of his own. He was more than an actor; he was a liar, a man who lied on principle. His original error had been a belief that he could without injury to himself split his honor into two parts, that in the interests of a supposedly higher honor he could dishonorably misrepresent himself to the anarchists with whom he foregathered. But these anarchists were human beings like himself, however misguided they might be, and in dishonorably gulling and betraying them he had inflicted an irreparable injury upon his own moral nature. In consequence, his imagination became diseased and played tricks on him: instead of furnishing him insight into the character of Lady Amateur, it created for him a false image of her, so inconsistent with the facts of her real nature that the lady he loved was forced to repudiate him.

Chapter 20.

THE SECRET AGENT

THE EVIL which Conrad isolated and examined in THE
INFORMER by means of the character Comrade Sevrin
reappears in his following short novel THE SECRET
AGENT (1906) —but in a purer and more distilled form,
less complicated by extraneous factors. Adolph Verloc, in
THE SECRET AGENT, is like Sevrin a police spy masquerading as an anarchist. Verloc, however, has no convictions; he likes his work not because he believes in its great
value to society but because he wants to earn his living as
effortlessly as possible and because he loves secrecy and deception for the subjective sense of superiority it gives him
over the people from whom he withholds knowledge about
himself. Sevrin on the other hand believed that he himself
practised deception only as a necessary strategy in furthering
the interests of a high ideal.

Verloc lives five separate simultaneous lives: husband and
family man, shop-keeper, member of a secret anarchist society, spy for the London police, and spy in England for
the German Government. None of the people who know
him in one of these roles know him in the other four; some
persons know him two or three of these roles, and some
few in even four of them, but no one knows him in all five.
The secret knowledge in Verloc that he has these other lives
unknown to his associates acts like an artificial stimulant,
a drug, on his self-conceit. That is where he establishes his
pride, in the solitary recesses of his ego, and his story is the

retribution that comes to him for this illicit self-love, permitted ultimately to no man.

For eleven years Verloc has been in the employ of the German Secret Service, his assignment being that of spy upon the activities of the international anarchists whose headquarters are in London. He has managed to become a trusted member of the anarchist organization and to report all anarchist plots to the German Embassy without drawing upon himself the plotters' suspicion that he is an informer. He is, on the other hand, highly esteemed by the plotters because he is the only one of their number whom the London police do not watch and occasionally molest. The anarchists attribute this to Verloc's astuteness in successfully concealing his anarchist affiliations; they never suspect the truth—which is that Verloc purchases his immunity by acting as an informer for the London chief of police.

For seven years Verloc has been married to Winnie, an English girl whose mother had kept the rooming house in which Verloc had lived. The mother and Winnie and Winnie's half-wit brother Stevie live with Verloc in a second floor apartment above a shop in which Verloc sells various household necessities. Winnie never suspects that the greater part of her husband's income is derived from another source than that of the shop. Verloc has never told his wife of his connection with the German Secret Service, nor that the radical-talking men, the cronies with whom he spends an occasional evening in a back room behind the shop, are active revolutionary anarchists.

Winnie had loved another man but had married Verloc because he, better than the man she loved, could take care of Stevie, the half-wit brother of whom she is passionately fond. For Stevie's sake, Winnie has been a good and faithful wife to Verloc.

Verloc likes his life precisely because of its loneliness. He shares only parts of his life with his associates; with none

of them, not even Winnie, does he share all of it. The old
German Ambassador knows more about Verloc's separate
lives than does anyone else, but even from him Verloc conceals his surreptitious dealings with Chief Inspector Heat of
the London police. Secretiveness, unsuspected by those clos-
est to him, makes Verloc feel like a god, omniscient in
comparison with his deluded associates.

A new German Ambassador, however, comes to London
and prods Verloc out of his easy ways. Whereas the old
Ambassador had been content merely to checkmate the plots
of the anarchists, Vladimir his successor desires to goad the
anarchists into some violent act which will incite the British
Government to suppress the organisation. He orders Verloc
to bomb the Greenwich Observatory.

This change of tactics on the part of his superiors dismays Verloc, but he cannot afford to disobey the order. His
secret connections with the London police make it inadvis-
able that he himself plant the bomb, and he therefore decides to make use of his boy Stevie, his half-wit brother-in-
law. One afternoon he takes Stevie for a walk in the park,
gives him a bucket in which, unknown to Stevie, a time-
bomb lies concealed, and directs him to carry the bucket
over to the Observatory wall, set it down and leave it there.
But on his way across the park, Stevie stumbles and falls; the
bomb explodes and Stevie is blown to pieces.

A bit of his collar-band, on which Winnie had written
Stevie's address, is found by the police. They come to Verloc's shop, find Winnie there and tell her what has happened
to Stevie.

When Verloc returns, he tells Winnie the complete story
of his life as a secret agent. He feels that he is compelled to
do this in order to explain in adequate detail the fatal accident which had caused Stevie's death. But Winnie hears
nothing that he says: her ear-drums are pounding with the
words "this man has murdered my Stevie." While he lies

on the couch talking, revealing his whole inner self for the first time to another human being, Winnie creeps up behind him and plunges a butcher-knife into his throat.

Loss of power to communicate effectively with his wife Winnie, or even to make himself partially comprehensible to her, was the penalty Verloc suffered for his lifelong self-indulgence in the conceit of secrecy. He had unwittingly dug such a deep gulf between himself and her and thereby created such a great distance between their minds that even his supreme and ultimate effort to bridge it could but fail. She had become as incomprehensible to him as he had to her. The loneliness which he had cultivated and reveled in had deprived him of the power to fathom, in his hour of need, the mind and motives of the one person who held his life in her hands. Verloc the masquerader, the masked man, by his success in divorcing appearance from reality had separated himself from others to such a degree that he was totally unable to re-establish contact. His secretiveness had resulted in total separation from the group, and of this the result was death.

One of the minor characters in this novel remains long in the memory as a symbolic image or epitome of the one subject about which all of Conrad's writings cluster: the social deviant. He is named "The Professor" because he is the most intellectual of the anarchists and because "the lamentable inferiority of his whole physique was made ludicrous by the supremely self-confident bearing of the individual." Conrad also says about him that "the extreme, almost ascetic purity of his thought, combined with an astounding ignorance of worldly conditions, had set before him a goal of power and prestige to be attained without the medium of arts, grace, tact, wealth—by sheer weight of merit alone."

The source of his self-confidence is no secret: everyone, including the police, knows that the Professor carries a detonator in his vest attached to enough explosive in his pocket to destroy everything within sixty yards, including, of course, himself. He is a small man with a cocky walk, but the police never dare to arrest him, because he has them convinced that his scorn of a world which has not recognized his merit has turned him into a desperate man, one who would not hesitate an instant to press the detonator button should anyone make one hostile move towards him.

The emotional attitude towards society embodied in this Conradian character represents but one of many patterns which can be formed from the elemental pieces in Conrad's problem. The amusing picture of a man who is at war with all other men and who has found a way to force all other men to keep their distance not only crystallizes one solution to the problem that Conrad dealt with but also defines that problem. The nerves that quiver in Conrad converge into the synapse that is the Professor, and in so doing they create a character who is an embodied image of one of Conrad's moods, one in which he entertained visions of impulsive and violent solutions to his oppressive problem.

Chapter 21.

THE DUEL

In THE DUEL (1906) Conrad looks at his problem from a direction diametrically opposite to that from which he looked at it in THE INFORMER and THE SECRET AGENT. It is as though he had walked all the way round to its other side and is now looking at it from the west instead of from the east. Whereas in THE INFORMER and THE SECRET AGENT we see men who lose themselves by secret acts of hostility to groups of which they are members, in THE DUEL we see a man who persists quixotically, even at the risk of violent death, in conforming to the exactions of a social custom which is not only obsolescent in the society of his time but also entirely obsolete in his own personal value-system. D'Hubert of THE DUEL helped to prolong the life of a social custom, and therefore of a society, which he knew to be dying and which he believed deserved to die, whereas Sevrin and Verloc helped to quell social groups struggling to be born. Conrad metes out defeat and death to Sevrin and Verloc while to D'Hubert he grants a long and happy life, and in this way he affirms the positive values of social cohesion, the centripetal as opposed to the centrifugal forces.

In choosing to tell the story of d'Hubert, Conrad would seem to have been moved by its aptness in putting the case for conformity in an extreme and therefore most deeply cut and sharply outlined form: d'Hubert is willing, against the grain, to conform not only to a social custom in which he

believes but even to one which he despises. D'Hubert felt
that social customs are the cement which holds society together, and so long as there was even one man remaining
alive who still gave allegiance to a once prevalent social
custom, response must be given to that man's invitation to
participate with him in observing that custom.

The custom in question is that of duelling to settle a
point of honor. Lieutenants d'Hubert and Feraud are officers in Napoleon's army and during their military career
both are advanced to Captain's rank, then to Colonel's, finally to General's. Over a period of two decades these men
fight five deadly duels with each other, Feraud being the
challenger every time. Feraud is culturally slightly behind
the times, in that it has never occurred to him that the duel
is an anachronistic institution; while d'Hubert is slightly
ahead of his time, in that the duel seems to him a somewhat
comical and irksome cultural left-over, now held in respect
only by the callow and the immature.

The first duel between these two men occurs when both
are young lieutenants. D'Hubert has been sent by his commanding officer to tell Lieutenant Feraud to place himself
under close arrest because the family of a civilian whom
Feraud had killed in a duel had registered a complaint
against him. D'Hubert is merely obeying orders when he
traces Feraud to the drawing-room of a lady upon whom he
is making a social call, but Feraud takes such offense at
d'Hubert for having cut short his visit with the lady that
he immediately challenges him to a duel. D'Hubert feels
that the challenge is unjustified, because his delivery of the
General's message had not been a personal affront on his
part to Feraud; but, since the unjustified challenge is in
itself a personal affront on Feraud's part to him, he accepts
the summons and fights the duel.

Feraud is wounded in the duel and d'Hubert as well as

Feraud is therefore placed under close arrest. The army is soon called into action, however, and both men are released.

Neither during their confinement nor during the ensuing campaign do either d'Hubert or Feraud reveal to their associates the cause of the dispute between them. This secrecy arouses the curiosity of their fellow officers and gives rise to much speculation; d'Hubert's reason for refusing to do any explaining is simply that he does not want to further humiliate Feraud by exposing the triviality of the offense which had angered him, while Feraud's reason is that he is afraid he will be laughed at. The mystery therefore grows until the hostility between the two men has become celebrated throughout the entire regiment.

Feraud responds to his friends' questions about the duel with merely a series of virulent vituperations against d'Hubert, general denunciation containing no specific charge and intended to discourage further inquiry, but he has by their means lashed himself into such a fury against d'Hubert by the time the campaign is over that he challenges d'Hubert to a second duel. This time Feraud is the victor, although d'Hubert is only slightly wounded. Another official inquiry results again in the refusal of both men to divulge the cause of the duel.

Feraud's anger is aroused a third time when d'Hubert is promoted to Captain's rank. Since duels between officers of unequal rank are forbidden, Feraud declared that d'Hubert had, by toadying to his superior officers, gotten himself a Captaincy because he was afraid to fight another duel. As soon as Feraud becomes a Captain, he challenges d'Hubert to a third duel. Both men are wounded and the fight is a draw.

A few years of campaigning in the Napoleonic wars now keep them apart. They meet again during the retreat from Moscow, marching back in the same group. Both are now

Colonels, but d'Hubert is made a General when they arrive
in Paris. When Feraud finally becomes a General too, d'Hubert, wounded, is convalescing in the south of France.

After the fall of Napoleon, d'Hubert is not included in
the mass arrest and prosecution of the Napoleonic Generals,
because Feraud has so often, from mere spitefulness, accused
him of not loving Napoleon that d'Hubert has come to be
considered a friend of the New Regime. Feraud himself,
however, was among the twenty Generals condemned to be
shot. This displeases d'Hubert, since it implies that Feraud
had been a more important personage in the Napoleonic
entourage than he. At considerable personal risk, d'Hubert
therefore intervenes on Feraud's behalf in the Judges' cham-
bers, with the utmost secrecy, and succeeds in saving Feraud's
life. The Judges reduce him to half pay and station him in
a small town in southern France.

Sometime later, Feraud learns that General d'Hubert has
been recalled to active service. This so infuriates him that
he journeys to d'Hubert's residence and challenges him to
a fifth duel.

D'Hubert is more intensely annoyed at this challenge
than he had been at any of the others, because he is about
to be married and is therefore anxious to avoid taking any
risk which might arouse rumors of scandal. He is enraged
at Feraud for hounding him at this late date with another
frivolous demand that he risk his life to satisfy a fancied
affront to an anachronistic concept of honor. D'Hubert has
in fact never shared Feraud's faith in the mystic virtue of
the duel as a means of establishing one's honor; he had
fought the first four duels as though they were a chore which
was being thrust upon him by a fanatic devotee of a van-
ishing code of manners, a chore which his own lingering
respect for the antique conventions still alive in the person
of Feraud compelled him to perform.

For the fifth time he cannot reject the old claim of the

dead code. He meets Feraud in a grove, the two of them entering simultaneously from opposite sides and each having an allowance of two shots with a pistol. They stalk each other among the trees, and d'Hubert succeeds in tricking Feraud into shooting twice and missing both times. D'Hubert therefore now possesses the right to shoot twice at an unarmed man, but he keeps his two shots in reserve and tells Feraud to go home and hold himself in perpetual readiness to pay the forfeit of his life which he now owes to his old enemy, d'Hubert.

A year later, when a son is born to d'Hubert, he sends a message to Feraud giving him back his life; and when Feraud's pension is cancelled, d'Hubert secretly furnishes the French government with funds to continue the regular and customary remittances during the remaining lifetime of his old enemy.

In d'Hubert, Conrad has given us a tender and affectionate portrait of a man who possesses the best characteristics of the true "conservative," a man who feels that he cannot, without belittling himself, fail to grant respect and esteem to those forms of the past which confront him with a retained flicker of their old strong life. D'Hubert fought those duels for the sake of that past time in which the duel was an important institution, passionately believed in. He himself was a modern unbeliever, for whom the duel was a dead form, but so long as there was a man yet alive for whom the duel had emotional meaning and so long as that man chose him for his opponent, d'Hubert felt that he owed the institution, if not the man, the satisfaction it desired. This is an entirely admirable feeling, and I believe that Conrad intended by means of d'Hubert to make us understand the emotional motives which underlie the persistent reluctance of the conservative mind to refuse obeisance to any form of past life which yet remains unextinguished. D'Hubert was an inarticulate soldier and could not tell what it was that constrained him to fight that last duel with Feraud; he merely knew that whatever it was 'twas even stronger than his adoration for the young girl he was about to marry. He had to obey that call even if he lost his life and destroyed the happiness of the girl who loved him. He felt as by intuition that the present time would lose its vigor if it denied any claim levied upon it by a past culture with enough life in it to express a claim.

Chapter 22.

GASPAR RUIZ

In GASPAR RUIZ (1906) Conrad returns from the periphery
of his theme to very near its center: the outcast attempting
to effect re-entry into the society which has thrust him into
outer darkness. However, Gaspar bears a curious resemblance
to d'Hubert in that both men seem to have a sense of funda-
mental kinship with their enemy. Gaspar in fury tries to
blast and hammer his way into the hearts of his enemies;
and d'Hubert, after having been pursued by Feraud as by
a recurring nemesis throughout nearly a lifetime, secretly
supports him. Both men seem to feel indebted to their
enemies, to need them, as though they were not merely outside them as observers but contained them within.

This ambivalence is re-enforced in Gaspar's case by
his dual and therefore ambiguous status as a citizen: he is
simultaneously the greatest outlaw in his nation (Chile) and
the most powerful supporter of the lawful order which the
Chilean secession from Spain was overthrowing. Furthermore, his situation derives its deepest complexity from his
desire to be fighting against, instead of for, the side which
he is supporting. His ferocity is like that of a rejected lover.

Gaspar Ruiz is a gigantic peasant who has been con-
scripted into the revolutionary army during the Chilean War
of Independence. He was subsequently captured in battle
by the Spanish Loyalists, forced by them to fight in their
ranks, and had then been recaptured by the Rebels and
condemned by them to be shot as a deserter.

Gaspar's strength is so great that, when the window bars of the guardhouse prove to be too close together to permit a bucket of water to be handed in to the suffocating prisoners, he bends the thick irons apart with his bare hands. The deserters, Gaspar among them, are led out to face the firing squad at dusk. All are shot and killed except Gaspar who, although he falls with the others, is only wounded. He lies still, feigning death until after the firing squad leaves, then crawls away in the dark to a nearby farmhouse where he asks for help. He is taken in by the two persons who live there, an old man and his daughter Erminia, who had once been rich but have been ruined by the Revolution and therefore hate the Rebels.

Erminia nurses him back to health and at his request apprises a friendly Rebel officer, who had tried to save him from execution as a deserter, of his miraculous escape from death and of his desire to enlist again in the Rebel army. This officer intercedes for him with the General, who, however, decides to recapture Gaspar and carry out the sentence of execution against him.

During the surprise raid organized by the General an earthquake demolishes the house. Erminia's father is killed, but Gaspar saves the lives of Erminia and the General by kicking open a jammed door of the crumbling house. He is rewarded by being permitted to escape from the General's raiding party. Having fallen in love with Erminia, he takes her with him to a distant city, the headquarters of the Revolutionary forces.

There he goes into hiding, writes a letter to the Commander-in-Chief of the Rebel forces protesting against the unjust charge that he is a deserter when he had in fact been a prisoner of war compelled to fight in the enemy's ranks, and asks for an opportunity to prove his loyalty. He is thereupon put in charge of a small body of men and sent into enemy territory to destroy an ammunition dump. Carrying out this assignment with speed, brilliance, and daring, he is promoted to Captain and sent to guard the southern frontier.

Erminia accompanies him to the outpost city and there she and Gaspar celebrate their marriage. Since Erminia is known to be not sympathetic to the Rebel cause, the civil governor objects to the wedding. He conspires against Gaspar and tampers with his officers. This so infuriates Gaspar that in a fit of uncontrollable rage he kills the governor.

This act makes him an outlaw, for the Chilean government charges him with murder and treason and sends a detachment of soldiers to arrest him. The men in his own small army, however, having come to idolize Gaspar, surround the government troops and destroy them.

Gaspar now leads his men into Indian territory and persuades the Indian tribes to join him in war against the Chilean Rebel armies. Erminia rides with him and helps to direct the campaigns. She instills into Gaspar, who worships her, some of her intense hatred of the Revolutionaries whose War of Independence had ruined her father, and together they lay waste two provinces, capture ships in the name of Spain, and wage such desperate war against the Rebels that the Spanish Government recognizes Gaspar's services by making him an officer of the Spanish Army.

This legitimizes Gaspar and elates Erminia; they now no longer consider themselves outlaws but lawful military representatives of a sovereign State, engaged in suppressing a treasonable rebellion. The Chilean Rebel Government, however, still considers them outlaws. The war with Spain has been virtually won and the independence of the State of Chile is soon recognized by the mother country.

Gaspar and Erminia refuse to acknowledge the Treaty and continue to carry on the war in the name of Spain. Erminia's demoniac hatred of the Rebels, that of an aristocrat with family ties in the mother country against the ris-

ing bourgeoisie of the colonial upper classes who have used
him as a mere tool in their war for freedom from foreign
landlords, spur the two of them on to a fierce and suicidal
conflict with the new order.

Theirs is a doomed cause, however. The entire Chilean
army is released by the Treaty with Spain for use as an ex-
peditionary force to close in on Gaspar and his Indian
allies. Erminia is captured by a treacherous ruse and imprisoned in an outpost fortress. Gaspar has a cannon dragged
from his headquarters to the fortress in order to break
down the doors of the stockade, but the gun carriage is lost
on the way. Gaspar has his men strap the cannon to his
back so that crouched on his hands and knees he serves as
a human platform for the great gun. The recoil of the third
shot breaks his back.

The manner of his death very fittingly symbolizes the
entire struggle of his life, which had been one long attempt
to relieve his isolation by battering his way in to the company of people from whom he had been excluded. His great
size and strength had been the first cause of his loneliness,
since it set him apart from other men. But his ejection
from the Rebel Army by court martial and sentence of
death before the firing squad had been so ignominious, absolute, summary, and unjust that the spiritual trauma it
inflicted on his simple, peasant, and uncomprehending mind
was more deadly than the physical wound he received. And
the rebuff he suffered when his pathetic offer to re-enlist
was answered by a second attempt to incarcerate and execute
him thrust him even further off into isolation.

Dogged courage, however, and his great need to effect re-
entry into the only society known to him drives him to per-
sist in battering his way back into the good graces of the
Rebel Army. The degree of desperation and loneliness afflicting him can be gauged by the fact that it was to the top

Commander-in-Chief of the Rebels that he directed his appeal.

The success of this stroke against great odds inaugurated for him a period of happiness and of respite from bitter isolation. The soldiers he commands love him and heartily accept him as their leader, the High Command of the Rebel Army has confidence in him, and Erminia consents to become his wife.

The snubs of the class-conscious civil governor, who resents sharing his authority with a peasant lout, soon give Gaspar notice, however, that once again discriminations are being made against him. Furthermore, he senses that his wife Erminia, immensely his superior in education and breeding, loves him only with her will and not with her heart, and that she only partially belongs to him. He knows that she had married him not because of his intrinsic merit but because the misfortunes of war had cast her adrift. The intensity of her passion is consumed not in loving him but in hating the Revolution which had destroyed her position and ruined her father's life.

Gaspar's physical assault on the civil governor was the result not only of a subconscious desire on his part to fight against the people whom his wife hated but also of his desperate rage at the loneliness which was oppressing him. And the war which he then carried on with such ferocity against the Rebel Armies was in fact an extended and post-marital courtship of his wife; only incidentally was it a fight put up by a fugitive from justice or a Loyalist attempt to hold the colony for Spain.

A child was born to him by Erminia shortly before her capture and imprisonment in the outpost fortress, and that child became for Gaspar the one human being of whom he could say "she at least is mine." Having been repulsed in his every effort to escape from his spiritual solitude into some emotional contiguity with others, he was at last reduced to the mere hope that his own child would wholeheartedly accept him. Bearing the great gun on his back in a Herculean and suicidal effort to recover possession of the only being on earth whom he thought might someday befriend him, Gaspar spent the last of his great strength.

Chapter 23.

IL CONDE

THE NEUROTIC overtones in the later behavior of Gaspar Ruiz appear again and in greater strength in the next story Conrad wrote: IL CONDE (1907). Whereas Gaspar, in a suicidal rage, continues to carry on a personal war with society after the official war had been ended by a Treaty, the Count on the other hand, in IL CONDE, disdains to contend with the society which contains elements hostile to him, preferring instead complete separation from the group and death in solitude. The primary fact in the lives of both Gaspar and the Count is the tension between themselves and the society about them, and both react against society in extreme rather than in moderate manners, but the Count's reaction in choosing death-without-a-struggle is a more severe condemnation of society than Gaspar's choice of a fight-to-the-death. Resentment against injustice in GASPAR RUIZ deepens into a black mood of despair in IL CONDE.

The incident with which the latter story opens occurs in Naples on a deserted promenade leading off a park where thousands of people are listening to a band concert. An insolently evil but well-dressed young man robs the Count, a refined and well-bred, elderly man, of all his pocket money. The young man uses a stiletto with which to threaten and intimidate his victim.

Later on in the evening, the Count discovers a gold piece in a stray pocket and with it buys himself a dinner in a restaurant. He suddenly catches sight of the young robber dining at a nearby table. The Count watches him eat, sees with what arrogance he calls for a cigar, and notices the deferential attitude of the waiters towards him. The Count's waiter informs him that his young neighbor is the leader of a secret society of university students and that he comes from a well-to-do family in the city. When the young robber finishes his meal he strolls over to the Count, brutally accuses him of being a cheat and a liar since he had apparently withheld a gold piece from him to whom he had pretended a few moments ago that his pockets had been completely emptied.

The utter viciousness of the young man's treatment of him so unnerves and appals the aged Count that, although the climate of no other city will keep him alive, he leaves Naples forever. He feels that for some incomprehensible reason he has been singled out for molestation by the criminal banded youth of Naples and that the indignities to which he has already been subjected have spoiled his beloved city for him.

The young robber is incarnate and absolute evil, and against it the old man has no desire to fight. He prefers to let evil have the victory and be permitted to gain full possession of an earth on which such evil can be encountered. His story expresses an attitude toward evil which, as a moody and emotional revulsion to its tiresome intrusion in our lives, comes no doubt to all of us sometime in our time.

Chapter 24.

THE BRUTE

THE STORY named THE BRUTE, which follows IL CONDE, sinks to yet a deeper depth of gloom and records yet a blacker mood than does IL CONDE. Everything external to the person, not only society but even brute matter itself, the material of which all physical objects are composed, is felt to be evil, hostile, and malevolent. By extension, the enmity between the person and society is conceived to subsist also between the person and the material constitution of the earth, inanimate nature itself.

In THE BRUTE (1908), a family by the name of Apse, having been successful shipbuilders for many generations, decide to build a masterpiece of a ship, sparing no expense, and name it *The Apse Family*. It is meant to be their crowning achievement, to embody all of their accumulated knowledge and craftsmanship, and to be free from the skimping suffered by the ships which they build to their customers' specifications. This one is to be owned by themselves, will bear their name, and must therefore be constructed with the best and heaviest materials and contain the finest and costliest accoutrements known to ships.

When it is finally launched, however, its crew finds the handsome, new ship to be almost unmanageable. Only with the greatest difficulty can *The Apse Family* be made to obey its sails and rudder. It lurches, staggers, changes its course unexpectedly, and is soon nicknamed "The Brute" by the men who sail it. Before long it acquires the reputation of killing a man on every trip.

The Apses continue stubbornly to insist, however, on sending the ship out to sea on voyage after voyage, and they grow ever more proud and sensitive about their ship while its reputation among seamen sinks continually lower. Captain Colchester does not like "The Brute," but he dare not incur the anger of the Apses by refusing to sail their ship. Neither do two of the younger men in the Apse organization, Ned and his brother Charles, dare refuse their appointments as first and second mates. Ned's first voyage as apprentice seaman, a few years previous to this appointment, had been on "The Brute" and he had seen a fellow apprentice flung out of the sails by a lurch of the ship before she left the dock. The boy had been killed.

Charles and Ned determine to work together as fellow officers in an attempt to break the ship of its bad habits and to lose not a man on the trip. Charles is in love with Captain Colchester's niece Maggie, who is to be a passenger on this voyage.

The trip is successful. Not a man is lost and Charles has become engaged to marry Maggie. But as they near the London docks at the end of the voyage, an anchor arm catches Maggie around the waist and drags her to the bottom of the Thames. Charles has a bout of brain fever, goes to the China seas and never returns to England; Captain Colchester's hair turns white in a few days and he refuses to take the ship to sea again except to scuttle her in the North Sea.

The Apse family still refuse to dismantle the ship. They hire another captain and crew, and send "The Brute" to sea again. The time has come, however, when only the most inferior and neediest sailors can be persuaded to man the disreputable vessel, now known to be a killer. As a direct result of the careless, negligent seamanship of the incompetent Captain, *The Apse Family* drove head on to a rocky coast one night and sank.

The occasional and unpredictable recalcitrance of matter, of brute nature, to man's shaping hand defeats this greatest effort of the master shipbuilders to form from wood an obedient beast of burden, just as the vein of intractability in human nature sometimes produces such completely evil beings as the young Napolitan robber in IL CONDE, Captain Brown in LORD JIM, or Jones in VICTORY. "The Brute" was Nature's revenge on the arrogance of man, on that vainglory which exults in taming and triumphing over the material world from which we rashly deem ourselves separate and elevated.

Chapter 25.

THE ANARCHIST

A HINT of recovery from the deep gloom which pervades his last several stories appears in Conrad's next short story, "The Anarchist" (1908) . While the anarchist Crocodile Paul makes the same hopeless choice as does the Count in IL CONDE, that of total rejection of society, he differs from the Count in that he seeks and finds in solitude a happiness which is the opposite of the death that the Count found there. It is as though Conrad had recalled, with a sense of relief, that by throwing off the restrictions of the group an individual can achieve anonymity as well as death and that anonymity can at least provide freedom, which is in itself desirable. Thus a ray of light arrives to relieve somewhat the blackness which total separation from the group has in the preceding stories been considered to be.

Crocodile Paul, unlike Gaspar Ruiz, does not fight against his loneliness: he relishes it and refuses to leave the tiny island where, in the mouth of a river on the East coast of South America, he lives in solitude.

Crocodile Paul had once been a good, steady worker in a French city. One night he got drunk in a tavern and was persuaded by some pranksters at a nearby table to shout a series of anarchist slogans. Soon the tavern was in an uproar, a riot took place, the police arrived, and many people were arrested. Paul was identified as the one who first began shouting the anarchist battlecries and he was therefore sen-

tenced not only as an inciter to riot but also as a revolutionary agitator.

When he is released from prison his record as an ex-
convict makes it impossible for him to secure any employment, and he is therefore forced to accept the assistance of
other ex-convicts who, masquerading as anarchists, carry on
their war against society by robbing banks. Once in their
clutches, he cannot escape from them. Having accepted
their food and companionship, compelled to do so since
no other is available to him, he is drawn against his wishes
into their enterprises and becomes a member of the gang.
Bank robbing cannot be carried on by one or two men
alone: it is an activity which requires several men and a
division of labor, and new recruits are therefore continually
needed by gang-leaders to replace those of their men whom
the police have caught. Paul is rescued from starvation by
two ex-convicts, Mafile and Simon, and then compelled to
stand watch for them while they rob banks.

The three of them are finally captured by the police and
sent to a penal colony off the coast of South America. Some
time later, during a prison break in which Paul takes no
active part, the three escape in a rowboat. Paul, however,
unknown to Mafile and Simon, has accidentally possessed
himself of a revolver. He hates the two men for having
taken advantage of his hunger and forced him into crime,
and he now gets his revenge. He forces them to row the
boat until a ship comes into sight, then he kills them. The
ship's crew takes him on board and permits him to swim
ashore as soon as they near land.

It is an island in the mouth of a river and is inhabited
only by the foreman of a farm and a few farmhands. The
foreman needs a mechanic to keep a motor boat in repair
and he hires Paul, nicknaming him "Crocodile" because he
prefers to live in the motor boat, apart from the other farmhands.

Several years later, Crocodile Paul tells his story to a visiting scientist, who befriends him out of a sympathetic curiosity concerning Paul's ability to lead so solitary a life without apparent discontent. Paul convinces the scientist that he wishes to stay on the island, apart from all society, for the remainder of his life. His motive is a desire to preserve his freedom: he fears that a return to any civilized society would result in his again losing his freedom either to people who would prey upon him, use him to further their own ends and exact an exorbitant price for providing him with food and shelter, or to the police who might discover his identity as an escaped convict. Crocodile Paul has learned the rock-bottom secret of happiness, but in doing so he had had to sacrifice forever all association with humankind. He is willing to accept solitude in order to secure the freedom which is necessary to happiness, because his life had taught him the intimate and necessary connection among these three things.

Chapter 26.

UNDER WESTERN EYES

UNDER WESTERN EYES (1909), like THE INFORMER
and THE SECRET AGENT, tells the story of a government
agent masquerading as a revolutionist in order to betray
the revolutionary group of which he is pretending to be a
member, but like AN ANARCHIST it differs from the
two earlier stories in that both Razumov, the secret agent
of UNDER WESTERN EYES, and Crocodile Paul of AN
ANARCHIST enter these groups not by choice but by the
duress of circumstances external to themselves. The four
stories have this in common: that they tell of men who,
like the Trojan horse in Troy, are filled with deadly hostility to the groups which contain them.

UNDER WESTERN EYES constitutes much the most
thorough exploration of the theme that the individual rather
than the group suffers destruction from his use of group-
membership as a cloak to keep the group from becoming
aware of the enemy in its midst and taking steps to guard
itself against his hostile actions. Razumov escapes destruction only by daring to tear the cloak off his own shoulders
and thus exposing himself to the group as its avowed enemy.
The thought residue at the very bottom of this theme
would seem necessarily to be that group-feeling in itself is
of such paramount value that for any individual to mimic it
for one evil group even in order to further the interests of
another good group is to destroy an element in himself essential to his existence as an individual. Conrad is attacking,

not deception in itself, but the delusion that an offense against group-feeling—as distinct from antagonism to a group—can be committed without the offender's own sense of group-feeling, and therefore himself suffering an irreparable injury. Both Comrade Sevrin and Adolph Verloc fall into this trap and are destroyed; Crocodile Paul avoids entrapment only by means of complete and hermit-like isolation from human society; and Razumov wrenches himself free from the trap at the expense of physical mutilation but spiritually intact at last.

Razumov first appears as a silent, scornful, superior, serious student at the University of St. Petersburg, with no family connections since he was the natural son of a great Prince who acknowledged the relationship only by supplying an allowance to his son through an attorney, and with no friends because he was intent on succeeding so well in his studies as to gain a professorship at the end of his term as student. His sole interests were philosophy and science, and the intellectual and academic career to which he looked forward.

Many of the serious students were anti-czarist social revolutionaries, but Razumov was not interested in politics. His aloof and preoccupied demeanour, so different from that of the care-free gaiety of the average student, led many of the revolutionaries to assume, however, that he was like themselves profoundly concerned about social injustice. Victor Haldin, one of the radical students, was so sure that Razumov, whom he knew but slightly, possessed deep revolutionary convictions that he wrote letters to his sister Nathalie, who lived in Switzerland, describing Razumov in glowing terms, thus leading her to believe that he is her brother's best friend.

Razumov, entirely unaware of this misconception of him with which Haldin and others have deluded themselves, is therefore appalled and infuriated when he returns home from classes one day and finds that his room has been selected by Haldin, who has just assassinated a tyrannical Czarist official, as a place of refuge from the police, and that his unwelcome visitor thinks him an astute and tight-lipped revolutionary who will eagerly help him to make his escape from Russia.

Since Haldin expresses such warm admiration for and such implicit trust in him, Razumov bides his time instead of immediately blurting out that he does not possess the revolutionary sympathies attributed to him. He consents to go, at Haldin's request, to a suburb of the city and inform a coachman by the name of Ziemianitch that Haldin will be waiting for him at a certain corner that evening and will expect him to be prepared to drive directly to the border. Razumov wants not only to get Haldin out of his room before the police find him there but also to avoid the hard and embarrassing task of defining himself to Haldin whose disappointment and chagrin would be so unsettling to them both. Haldin had misjudged Razumov, and Razumov could not correct the misjudgment without greatly embarrassing Haldin, doing so, moreover, at a time when Haldin is laboring under the great emotional exaltation of having that day achieved, as he thinks, a great revolutionary stroke in ridding the Russian people of a foul oppressor.

When Razumov finds Ziemianitch, however, the coachman is sodden drunk and cannot be roused. This so enrages Razumov that he beats the drunken man with a fork handle, and into that beating he puts all his rage not only against Ziemianitch for not being ready to remove the incriminating visitor from Razumov's room but also against Haldin for having misunderstood him and, by implicating him in the crime, endangered his future career as a quiet and intellectual professor of philosophy, and against all violence practised not only by revolutionaries but also by the oppressive autocracy.

Razumov's frenzy then takes him on his first visit to
his father, Prince K. The police are making a house to house
search for the assassin, and if they find him in Razumov's
room, Razumov will never be able to prove his innocence
or to maintain his true identity as a non-revolutionary intellectual. He desperately wants to protect the plan which
he has made for his life from being wrecked by Haldin's
interference and he is willing to sacrifice Haldin to the
police if by so doing he can continue on his own chosen
path.

Why did he not merely return to his room, explain himself to Haldin and ask him to leave? Why did he decide to
deliver Haldin to the police? Because the descent of Haldin
on him has made him realize that his chosen path is not
only non-revolutionary but anti-revolutionary. He believes
that the method of the assassin and of those who work for
the violent overthrow of the government would bring more
misery on many people than the oppressive government now
brings on a few; for that reason he deliberately chooses to
range himself on the side of the despotic government and
against the revolutionaries.

After Prince K. hears Razumov's story he sends for the
chief of police and has Razumov repeat his account in the
Chiefs presence. Razumov has omitted his visit to Ziemianitch, saying only that Haldin has an appointment to meet
a coachman at a certain corner and hour that evening. The
Chief tells him to go home and keep Haldin company until
the appointed time, when the police will pick up the assassin on his way to meet the coachman.

Razumov does so, spending several anguished hours listening to the doomed man tell of his revolutionary plans
for liberating the Russian people. Since he feels that his
own whole future career and his conception of his own role
in life is at stake, he steels himself to listen in silence to
the outpourings of Haldin's inmost thoughts.

The next day he attends his classes as usual, and several days later he hears that Haldin has been executed.

Razumov was mistaken, however, in thinking that his life would go on as though Haldin had never visited him. Haldin had spoken of Razumov to the other students so often and in such superlative terms that the names of the two men had become closely associated. Revolutionary sympathizers who have clerical jobs in government offices overhear Razumov's name connected with Haldin's in sundry official conversations and they consequently begin to spread rumors that Razumov had been Haldin's accomplice. The police become aware of the rumors and search Razumov's room one day while he is attending his classes. This becomes known to the students and greatly adds to the volume of conversation about him.

The police have found nothing incriminating in Razumov's room; in fact, they found fragments of writing which indicate a deep aversion to any kind of revolutionary violence. The rumor spreads among the students, however, that Razumov is about to be arrested, and many of them urge him to flee Russia at once.

Razumov has become a national revolutionary hero. His angry denials of having had anything to do with the assassination are taken to mean that for fear of the police he wants his part in the great deed to remain a secret. The police are the only ones who believe him, and Councillor Mikulin, the Chief, sees an opportunity to make great use of Razumov and his undeserved reputation.

He calls Razumov in to his office for several conferences and urges him to accept the role of revolutionary hero which has been forced upon him by the deluded radicals, and to accept also their offers of assistance in escaping from Russia. He can then, as a fully accredited conspirator, go among the plotters in their Switzerland headquarters, learn all their plans and report them to the Russian police. Mikulin points

out to him that his academic career is ruined anyway, since
the University authorities themselves will always, because
of his reputation among the radicals, suspect him of somehow having made it impossible for the police to prove his
real guilt. He can, on the other hand, become a very successful spy at once, since the conspirators will admit him, as
Haldin's associate, immediately into their inmost councils.
Furthermore, Prince K. urges Razumov to consent to Mikulin's offer of employment in the secret service. The argument that finally wins Razumov over is Mikulin's statement
that big reforms are about to be initiated for ameliorating
the conditions of the Russian peasants, but that these reforms
will be indefinitely postponed should there occur any further
outbreak of revolutionary violence; it is therefore very
urgent that outbreaks now being planned should be fore-
stalled. Razumov can forestall them by discovering the plans
of the plotters in Switzerland and forwarding the information to Mikulin. He will thereby be doing a great service to
the Russian people by helping to make possible the orderly
and gradual introduction of reform measures.

And thus it comes about that within a short time after
his life had been broken into by Haldin, Razumov gives
up his studies and his academic career in exchange for a new
life as police spy disguised as a revolutionary agent. The
student radicals arrange his escape from Russia, the police
pretend to give pursuit and thereby add verisimilitude to
his flight for safety, and the revolutionary groups in several
European cities welcome him as a heroic refugee from the
land of tyranny. He finally reaches the headquarters of the
Russian plotters in Switzerland and is immediately greeted
as an invaluable accession to the revolutionary general staff.

His position is further strengthened, presently, by the
suicide of Ziemianitch. If knowledge of his visit to Ziemianitch had by any chance reached either the police or the
revolutionaries, his having withheld that information would

have shaken everyone's confidence in him and led to further inquiries. The revolutionaries immediately assume that Ziemianitch must have been the one who betrayed Haldin to the police and that his suicide had been motivated by guilt and self-condemnation. The death of Ziemianitch and the hypothesis to which it gives rise completely cover Razumov's tracks and enable him to feel perfectly secure in his new role as trusted revolutionist and therefore successful counter-agent.

However, he becomes increasingly unhappy. He had thought that his political convictions and his resentment of Haldin would give him the strength to maintain two selves, the secret real one who had visited Ziemianitch and betrayed Haldin, and the public apparent one who had been Haldin's friend and associate. His political convictions do not weaken nor does he lose his resentment of Haldin, but he begins to despise himself for making use of an unfair advantage over his enemies, the revolutionists. The footing on which he moves among them is furnished by the false legend about him which they themselves have created, but he himself is conniving to maintain the false legend by suppressing certain facts about himself. That they have victimized themselves does not make it any the less true that he is also guilty of victimizing them. It makes him miserable that he cannot fight them openly, confront them with his real self instead of with this mere false image, his apparent self.

He goes on with his work, however, writing memoranda to Councillor Mikulin regularly and attending meetings of the revolutionary committees—until he meets, and falls in love with, Nathalie Haldin, the sister of the man whom he had betrayed to the police. Nathalie had idolized her brother, and since Victor had written her such glowing letters about him she is predisposed in Razumov's favor before she ever meets him and consequently transfers to Razumov the allegiance she had felt towards Victor. She is a trustful as well as a beautiful girl, and represents Razumov's greatest temptation to continue his career as a secret agent.

Nathalie's evident desire to marry him precipitates Razumov's great struggle with himself. He must decide either to marry Nathalie and thereby close the door forever to the possibility of revealing his secret and real self, the one who had murdered Victor Haldin, or on the other hand to abandon his career as secret agent. The death of Ziemianitch has made him safe from exposure, and marriage to Nathalie will be his reward for remaining apostate to his true identity.

His final decision, however, is that he must, at any cost, force the image of himself that he presents to the world and the image of himself which he possesses in his own mind to coalesce and become one. He feels that he can no longer endure a situation in which his true self is like a disembodied and invisible ghost which, instead of inhabiting his visible body, merely accompanies him wherever he goes.

Driven by the need to recover his true self and to destroy the apparition which he had permitted himself to become, he tells first Nathalie and then the assembled revolutionists that he, not Ziemianitch, had betrayed Victor Haldin. Before the revolutionists can decide what to do with him, Nikita, another police spy, takes Razumov aside and breaks his eardrums, deafening him for life. He wanders about all night alone, crazed with pain, is hit by a streetcar and badly hurt.

Nathalie becomes a social worker in Central Russia, and Razumov returns to a small town in the south of Russia. He has not long to live and is both crippled and deaf, but he is not unhappy. Some of the revolutionists even visit him occasionally, because they respect him for having had the courage to declare himself openly to them without having come to share their political and intellectual convictions.

Chapter 27.

THE SECRET SHARER

OFFICIAL SOCIETY, represented by government officers and those in authority charged with law-enforcement, has been appearing at least in the background of several Conrad stories immediately preceding THE SECRET SHARER (1909). In this story, however, official society and its opposite, the outlaw, take the foreground. Conrad's earlier stories dealt with outcasts in conflict with orthodox groups, but a progression has occurred from Almayer and Willems through Lord Jim, Gaspar Ruiz, Verloc and Razumov to Leggatt, the murderer and outlaw of THE SECRET SHARER.

This is of course a natural progression, since the archetype of all groups is the ruling governmental society of any land, and the extreme type of the outcast or the deviant individual is the outlaw. With this story Conrad has finally isolated his antinomies, the individual who is a law unto himself, and the authority of law and order which stands for organized mankind.

The inescapable fact about THE SECRET SHARER is that in this story Conrad himself, the ship-captain in the story, chooses to conceal a murderer from his pursuers and assists him to escape capture by the legal authorities. Furthermore, this man who helps a fugitive from the law is himself an officer of the law, having just been appointed captain of a ship, his first command, and this act of law-evasion is his first act in his new post. Knowing that a crime has been committed, the captain assists and shelters the offender with the intent to defeat justice and in doing so he becomes an accessory after the fact.

The murderer, Leggatt, and the captain had held identical jobs as mates on separate ships until a few weeks previous to Leggatt's criminal act and the captain's promotion to his first command. And the captain realizes that the crime that Leggatt had committed was a crime that in similar circumstances he himself might have committed, and instead of becoming a member of the ruling class on the high seas he easily might, like Leggatt, have deviated into the class of the hunted outlaw. He therefore identifies himself with the murderer rather than with the judges who would condemn Leggatt should he be brought before them in a court of law.

The young ship-captain meets Leggatt for the first time during his first night as captain. He has a feeling of inadequacy in facing up to his new duties and he therefore spends his first night in performing the duties of the night watchman whom he has sent to bed. He hopes to accustom himself to his new and elevated status by spending the night in solitude and contemplation on the deck of the ship of which he is the new master. The ship is anchored outside a harbor in the Java sea and is ready to sail on the following day.

During the night he notices that a rope ladder is hanging over the side of the ship, goes to pull it in, and finds a naked man floating in the water and clinging to the rope's end. He invites the swimmer to climb aboard.

The stranger, a young man, introduces himself by the name of Leggatt and tells his story in a low voice, after he has put on the sleeping suit which the captain has fetched for him. Leggatt says he had been swimming for a couple of hours and had come from the ship across the bay. He had been mate of that ship until seven weeks ago, when he had been confined to his cabin for having killed a member of his crew, a worthless wastrel of a sailor who had exasperated him by insolence after a long hard storm. Leggatt had grabbed the sailor by the throat just as a huge wave broke over the deck. When the water disappeared, Leggatt's fingers were still grappling the sailor's throat, and the sailor was dead. The captain had locked Leggatt in his cabin and had intended to turn him over to the land authorities. Leggatt, however, had this evening, the first time that the ship has approached land, escaped from his cabin and jumped overboard. He had intended to swim until he sank, rather than face the routine of an Official Inquiry, but had come upon this neighboring ship in the dark, noticed the rope ladder and decided to cling to it for a short rest.

The captain, who narrates the story, and Leggatt seem to understand each other perfectly. The captain feels that under the same circumstances he himself would have done what Leggatt did, and he cannot disapprove of Leggatt's wish to disappear rather than face the Court of Inquiry. He himself has often been tempted to take some worthless sailor by the throat and no doubt would have done so had he been provoked to the same extent as had Leggatt. He proceeds to hide the refugee in his cabin and protect him from pursuit. It is as though he were protecting himself from the consequences of something which he himself might very well have done.

The next morning the captain of Leggatt's ship arrives and tells his story. He is astonished and suspicious at not finding Leggatt on board, but he accepts the assurances of the narrator-captain that none of his men had seen the runaway mate.

Several nerve-wracking days follow this event. Leggatt hides in the captain's shower-room when the steward is making the stateroom tidy; he and the captain converse only in whispers and only at night; the captain notices that the crew has begun to show in their behavior towards him that they think he is acting queerly. He comes upon groups of sailors whose sudden dispersal upon his approach indicates that they have been discussing him.

Leggatt soon decides that they have sailed far enough down the Java coast to be out of reach of the port authorities, who had undoubtedly been notified of his escape, and he therefore asks the captain to put his ship within swimming distance of the shoreline after dark. The captain is reluctant to do so, since he wishes to remove the secret sharer of his cabin as far as possible from the danger of recapture, but he agrees to Leggatt's proposal because the danger that some member of the crew will accidentally discover Leggatt's presence on shipboard is becoming too great. That night, on the pretext that he wants to pick up some land breezes with which to augment the ship's speed, the captain pilots his ship dangerously close to the shore line; Leggatt slips over the side in the dark and makes his getaway unseen.

The captain is now a changed man. His feeling of inadequacy has entirely vanished and he takes charge of his ship and crew in full confidence that he can body forth in his own person the full authority which his position of captain demands of him. It is as though the young captain before he could exercise authority convincingly to himself and to his men, had had first to take the law into his own hands and symbolically flout the authority of those above him before he could exert authority over those under him. The first use to which he put his newly acquired authority was that of shielding a fleeing outcast from a punitive society. The captain-narrator, Conrad himself, stands for the official group, and Leggatt stands for the deviant individual; and by protecting him from the other members of his group, Conrad here takes Leggatt's sin on his own shoulders and thereby admits not only his own moral complicity but that of society as well.

Chapter 28.

A SMILE OF FORTUNE

THE SECRET SHARER was written in a mood of strong fellow-feeling for the outcast, the man whom society has rejected, while the series of stories immediately preceding tended to emphasize the necessity for the individual, for his own sake, to come to terms with the social group with which he is involved. A further shift of emphasis, a note of caution and self-admonition, occurs in Conrad's next story, A SMILE OF FORTUNE (1910). In this story a young ship-captain's predilection to look with favor upon those whom some social group has elected to boycott misleads him into making such an emotionally biased instead of objectively correct appraisal of a certain person that he comes near to marrying a girl totally unsuited to him. The Achilles' heel in his nature is the existence in him of an almost overpowering impulse to throw himself into the scales on the side of persons whom official society had condemned and the subject of the story is his struggle to avoid the pitfall of self-immolation.

The young bachelor captain has been instructed by his ship's owners to stop at a certain tropical island in the Indian ocean, pick up there a small addition to his cargo, and make himself acquainted with a Mr. Ernest Jacobus, prominent merchant with whom the firm has had in the past some business dealings.

He drops anchor in the island's harbor very early one morning and is shortly thereafter astonished and mystified by the arrival from shore of a Mr. Jacobus whom he as-

sumes to be the prominent merchant. The captain treats his
visitor with great cordiality and respect and invites him to
breakfast on board ship—only to learn before the meal is
over that his guest is not the great merchant, Ernest Jacobus,
but his brother Alfred, a lowly ship chandler whose business
should properly be transacted with the ship's steward rather
than with the captain. This initial faux pas, due to his mistaking the identity of the first islander he meets, not only
makes the captain feel foolish, chagrined, disgruntled, and
somewhat out of temper, but it also implants in him a mood
which lasts as long as his stay on the island, a matter of two
or three weeks. The feeling that he has been taken at a disadvantage is strengthened by his learning, upon going ashore,
that Ernest, the merchant, and Alfred, the ship chandler,
haven't spoken to each other for eighteen years, and that
the islanders look upon Alfred with considerable moral
disapproval because of some blemish on his character.

The captain's first duty on shore is to attend the funeral
of a fellow ship captain's child and he learns from the be-
reaved father that the "wrong Mr. Jacobus," as he now
names him to himself, has been most helpful in making all
the funeral arrangements. Another captain is, however, in-
censed at the ship chandler for having tried to sell him some-
body else's cast off figurehead to replace the one lost from
his ship one night at sea. Alfred Jacobus attempts to place
all the visiting ship captains under some obligation to him
by taking advantage of every opportunity to do them some
service of which they stand in need. He is a resourceful busy-
body and his motive seems to be not merely a desire to sell
provisions and supplies to all the ships which have stopped
in the harbor but also to gain from passing strangers the
social approval which he is denied by his fellow townsmen.

In accordance with the instructions from his employers,
the captain (who is also the narrator of the story) presently
calls upon Mr. Ernest Jacobus, the prominent merchant.

The call is however a total failure. When the mulatto office boy, whom the captain had found in the outer office, goes in to Mr. Jacobus's inner office to waken his employer from an afternoon nap and notify him of the captain's presence, he is catapulted out again with kicks, cuffs and curses. This brutal treatment of a servant so incenses the captain against Mr. Jacobus that he cannot bring himself to talk civilly with the man and he therefore excuses himself almost immediately. On his way out he notices that the mulatto boy's physiognomy resembles that of Mr. Jacobus and he surmises that the boy must be Mr. Jacobus's natural son.

This evidence of a cavalier morality and an autocratic temper on the part of the respected and powerful Jacobus makes the captain think more favorably of the shunned and discredited brother. Partly as a gesture of displeasure with Ernest, he pays Alfred a friendly visit in his ship supply store. During the conversation Alfred makes two suggestions: that the captain buy, on his own account and for speculation, ten or fifteen tons of potatoes, and that he come to Alfred's house some evening for dinner.

The captain mentions the dinner invitation to some people of his acquaintance, a socially prominent family to whom he has had letters of introduction from mutual friends, and he is advised strongly against having social relations with Alfred Jacobus. He is told that the ship chandler had once been a respectable citizen, married and the father of a child, and partner in business with his brother Ernest, but that he had run off with a circus girl, followed her and the circus for a number of years, and had finally returned to the island bringing with him a baby daughter. His wife had died in the meantime and his first daughter had married a local physician. The presence of the girl, now over eighteen years of age, had kept the scandal alive and Alfred beyond the social pale. No one ever visits the home of Alfred Jacobus, a large old house within a walled garden, and the girl and her governess, a distant relative of the Jacobus's, never leave the house. The family is socially taboo.

However, the captain is not impressed with the warning. He is curious to see the girl whom nobody knows. When Alfred repeats his dinner invitation a few days later, in response to the captain's request for help in locating a supply of special and scarce bags needed in loading the ship's cargo, he accepts the invitation readily.

The captain meets Alice Jacobus, who turns out to be a sullen, stormy, petulant girl, rather beautiful but slovenly, who won't converse and who refuses to dine with her father and the captain. She does not, however, refuse to sit with the captain on the screened-in veranda off the walled garden when he calls at the house to spend his afternoons while waiting for Alfred to find the cargo bags. The unresponsiveness of the girl, her complete lack of formal schooling, her ignorance of the world outside the tiny tropical island, and her acceptance of social ostracism as the normal human life, excite the captain to exert himself in an effort to arouse Alice from her apathy. He remonstrates with her, cajoles and upbraids her, nicknames her "Miss Don't-Care," and finds himself falling in love with her precisely because she exasperates him. He takes her part and wishes to instill in her a desire to fight back against the adversity of her life. Nettled by the sight of her passive rebellion, he wants to see her give battle to the social powers on the island which have kept her cornered and cowed for so many years.

After many afternoons of futile effort to elicit some conversational response from the recalcitrant and contemptuous, silent girl, the captain tells her that his ship is nearly loaded and that he will be sailing away in two days. To his amazement Alice has a fit of the shivers and shows signs of terror. She breaks out into the words: "If you were to shut me up in an empty place as smooth all round as the palm of my hand, I could always strangle myself with my hair."

In the ensuing conversation he learns that what he had taken for her sullen and helpless resentment at the circumstances of her life had been in fact terror of himself personally, based on a supposition that her father, wanting to get rid of her, had employed the captain to be her abductor.

The accent of sincerity in his horrified denial of any such intention convinces her, whereupon her sullen rebellious manner vanishes and is replaced by a complete indifference to the captain. This transformation in the girl so exasperates him that he seizes and kisses her furiously many times. She consents to the kissing but runs off when she hears her father enter the house. Alfred comes out on the porch, notices Alice's shoe on the floor—she had lost it in the scuffle—picks it up and holds it in his hands while he broaches again the proposal that the captain buy ten or fifteen tons of potatoes for personal speculation. Feeling that Alfred suspects him of having been making love to Alice, and that the alternative to his buying the potatoes will be a demand that he marry Alice, the captain agrees to buy the potatoes.

Alfred immediaely goes out to load the potatoes on the captain's ship and the captain stays to have one more interview with Alice. She seems to be completely at ease with him now and voluntarily kisses him goodby as though she regrets his departure. The captain, however, discovers to his surprise that he no longer feels any thrill in her presence. This fact about himself dismays him, because it is conclusive proof that he had been for many days the dupe of his own imagination. Alice's charm for him had been real enough, but it had been inspired in him not by the actual girl as in herself she really was but by his misconception of the meaning of her behavior. He had imagined what state of mind he himself would have arrived at if he had had to live her life, of which he knew only a number of external facts; then he had imagined Alice as possessing and her behavior as expressing that state of mind. When Alice's exposure of her true state of mind reveals to him the great disparity between it and what he had thought it to be, her charm for him vanished.

The captain had conceived himself to be the champion of a social outcast, but he lost his role upon discovering that Alice's conception of her predicament, seen from the inside, differed so radically from what it appeared to be when seen from the outside, through the eyes of an observer. That he was a sympathetic observer proved to be no guarantee of his accuracy in understanding her. In fact, his emotional revulsion from the attitude of conventional society toward the girl had deprived him of the objectivity essential to sound judgment. His choleric and impulsive partisanship for the class of people rejected by a self-righteous society on shallow moralistic grounds had betrayed him into an emotional attachment to, almost into marriage with, a girl whose pathology would have rendered them forever exotic to each other.

Chapter 29.

FREYA OF THE SEVEN ISLES

In FREYA OF THE SEVEN ISLES (1910) Conrad again
delivers an attack on official society in defense of the individual. The principal thing that happens in the story is that an
irresponsible officer of the law perverts the power placed in
his hands by society from law-enforcement to personal vengeance. A police officer who in his private capacity is a jealous
and defeated lover uses his police power to take a vicious
revenge upon his rival, the successful lover, and thereby the
girl too. Conrad accentuates the identification of the opposing forces as being a pair of lone and innocent individuals
on the one hand and a group evil with power on the other
by making the individuals non-Dutch free-lance entrepre-
neurs in a Dutch Colonial area where their opponent represents all the oppressive power of an absentee imperialistic
ruler over subject peoples.

Lieutenant Heemskirk is commander of a Dutch gunboat on patrol duty in the waters adjacent to the Dutch
East Indies; Jasper Allen is the English owner of a beautiful
sailing brig engaged in light coastwise shipping; and Freya
Nielsen is the twenty-year old daughter of a former Danish
ship-captain who had retired and leased a small island from
the Dutch government on which to grow tobacco and also
to bring up Freya, whose English mother had died at sea.

Freya is an enticing sight to Heemskirk, who often stops
at the island to visit Captain Nielsen but whose real motive

is to look at Freya under cover of a pretense at conversation with her father.

Freya, however, is secretly engaged to marry Jasper Allen. Captain Nielsen does not approve of Jasper's visits to his house, because he is afraid that the Dutch authorities will look with disfavor upon him for showing hospitality to an English foreigner. Freya thinks it best, therefore, to keep her engagement to Jasper a secret from her father and, on her twenty-first birthday, to confront him with an elopement marriage.

Heemskirk's jealousy becomes aroused when he begins to notice Jasper Allen's brig frequently moored in the island harbor; and one day, coming into the Nielsen house unannounced, he catches sight of Jasper and Freya in each other's arms. This puts him into a rage that he manages to suppress until late that evening when he finds himself alone with Freya for a few moments. While Freya is playing the piano, he seizes her from behind and showers savage kisses on her. She slaps him so hard that he howls in rage and pain. Nielsen comes in at that moment, thinks that Heemskirk has been attacked by a violent toothache, urges him to bed and feeds him laudanum.

Heemskirk spends a sleepless night, hears Freya go out on the porch early the next morning, and through a crack in his door watches her wave goodby kisses to Jasper, whose brig is leaving the harbor. Freya, sensing Heemskirk's spying, purposely lets her dressing gown fall part way down her unclothed shoulders in order to further frustrate, tantalize and punish the man who had forced his unwelcome kisses on her. A short while later she takes her turn as an unseen watcher: from behind the curtains of her bedroom window she sees Heemskirk stumbling away towards the pier, a picture of enraged and baffled passion. She runs to the piano and plays loud ringing music as though she were hurling the sounds after him like parting shots.

Heemskirk's gunboat follows Jasper's brig, intercepts it as it is leaving a river in an area where armed natives had recently risen against the Dutch. Jasper is taken on board the gunboat, and a Dutch crew is sent to take possession of the brig, which is then attached by a towline to the gunboat. The pretense for the arrest is that all boats visiting the troubled area are being taken to Macassar for clearance against suspicion of gun smuggling to the natives.

On the way to Macassar it is discovered that Jasper's papers show registration of eighteen rifles in the ship's stores but that the rifles are not on the boat. Jasper's first mate confesses to having traded the rifles for liquor one night while drunk, but this evidence is suppressed by Heemskirk. The unexpected opportunity which the disappearance of the rifles gives him to trump up a plausible charge against Jasper in the Dutch courts emboldens Heemskirk to commit for vengeance sake a crime with little risk of retribution. When the gunboat is approaching a rocky reef near Macassar, Heemskirk surreptitiously loosens the towline to Jasper's brig—which then runs full tilt high up on the reef and is wrecked.

From the deck of the gunboat Jasper sees his beautiful brig, which was soon to have become Freya's home, running to its death on the rocks; he sees it strike and with horrified eyes he watches it shudder to a full stop and then totter as though mortally wounded. The shock sends him into a delirium from which he never fully recovers. Freya finally learns what had happened, falls ill with anemia and dies.

Heemskirk reports the loss of the brig as due to accidental breaking of the towline and is officially excused for the mishap as well as commended for having brought a gun smuggler to justice. He therefore, by perjuring himself, avoids punishment for the crime which his possession of police power enabled him to commit. He had contrived to make the private revenge which he inflicted on a personal opponent appear to be an unavoidable accident in the performance of his official duties, and had therefore perverted to personal uses powers which had been conferred upon him for official uses only. Since society is responsible for the actions of those to whom it delegates its authority, society itself is the villain of this story and a pair of innocent individuals are its tragic victims.

Chapter 30.

THE PARTNER

IN THE PARTNER (1910) we find a group composed of three men who have been associated with one another for a number of years in a business partnership which has supported its three members and their families better than any of the partners could have done had they worked alone. This social group is, however, brought to ruin and its individual members impoverished by an anti-social act on the part of one of its members. This story is therefore a defense of the group and an attack upon unsocial behavior on the part of an individual. In this instance the deviant individual breaks the supporting pillars of the group's shelter and brings its roof down in wreckage upon them all including himself.

The three partners, Cloete, George Dunbar and Harry Dunbar, own and operate a warehousing business in London and a freighter captained by Harry. An opportunity becomes available to Cloete to acquire controlling interest in an extremely lucrative patent medicine venture and he proposes to his partner George that the capital required by the new enterprise be obtained by wrecking the freighter for its insurance money. George is at first horrified by the indecent proposal, but he is finally prevailed upon to keep silent while Cloete persuades the unsuspecting Captain Harry to hire as first mate a man whom Cloete has secretly bribed to sink the ship. This man, Stafford, weakens one link of the anchor-chain and the ship is consequently driven up on a reef in the Channel during a storm. The ship's distress call is announced in London, and Cloete, accompanied by George and by Harry's wife, travel hastily up the coast to the little town from which rescue operations are being carried on. Cloete persuades the captain of one of the rescue tugs to let him go with the tug out to the stricken ship, which he then manages to board while the crew is being taken off. Stafford sees him and forthwith demands that his promised bribe be doubled. They quarrel and Cloete succeeds in locking Stafford in a cabin, leaving him there to go down with the ship. Captain Harry enters that cabin a little later and Stafford, mistaking him for George, kills him with a revolver he had found there.

The death of Captain Harry cuts in half the insurance money available to Cloete and George, since Harry's share goes directly to his widow in the form of an annuity. The balance of the insurance money was insufficient to enable Cloete and George to take any part in the patent medicine venture—which in later years fulfilled Cloete's early estimation of its value by making a huge fortune for its owners.

The fact that this thoroughly evil man does not become a social outcast but maintains his status as a man of good repute within the social order seems to serve, when considered in relation to other stories of Conrad's as an emphatic reminder that the two classifications of people, evil men and social outcasts, are by no means identical. Conrad seems to be saying that since here we have an evil man who is not a social outcast, perhaps the converse may occur: social outcasts who are not evil men.

Chapter 31.

PRINCE ROMAN

IN PRINCE ROMAN (1911) Conrad tells, with admiration, the story of a man who seceded from the group of which he was a member by right of birth and who therefore voluntarily chose ostracism and exile as a matter of principle. In this story intellectual integrity is opposed to social adjustment, and Conrad indicates his preference for the former. He holds up to view a man who was at peace with himself by reason of the fact that he had had the courage to affront a society of which he disapproved and to take the punitive consequences.

Prince Roman had been born into one of the Polish noble families which had accepted Russian domination over the Polish nation and had in return been left by the Czar in full possession of their landed estates. When young Prince Roman grows to manhood, however, he feels that his parents' acquiescence in the social system which permits a foreign strong nation to exact tribute from a neighboring weak nation is dishonorable. He therefore takes part in a Polish peasant revolution against Russia and is captured by the Czar's troops. His parents have influence at the Czar's court and obtain for their son the right to choose between freedom, to be purchased by a mere formal begging of the Czar's pardon, and servitude for twenty-five years in the salt mines of Siberia.

Prince Roman, however, announces in court during his trial that he had joined the rebels "from conviction"; he chooses the servitude, and spends the best twenty-five years of his life as an exile and convict, an outcast from the privileged society into which he had been born. Intellectual integrity had made a social outcast of Prince Roman, who chose to be at odds with society because he condemned it.

Chapter 32.

CHANCE

In CHANCE (1911) a marriage occurs between two persons in each of whom an outcast mentality had been induced by traumatic childhood experiences. The novel is a study of the effect which these two persons' low self-esteem has upon their marriage to each other. Both had felt unloved and rejected in early life and both have accepted in self-judgment the adverse verdict which they fancy society has pronounced against them. The similarity of their emotional predicaments draws them together into marriage but it also provides the pitfalls in which their marriage nearly perishes.

Both Flora de Barral and Captain Anthony consider themselves to be outside the pale which encloses those whose privilege it is to be wholly loved by a person of the opposite sex. Their self-depreciation, their conviction of their own unlovableness, causes them to cast themselves out from the society of others and even to found their marriage to each other on an agreement to maintain sexual abstinence not only from all others but also from each other. The plot of the novel consists of an account of the events in their lives which brought about this state of mind and of the events which eventually led to the disintegration of the wall which their mental and emotional predicaments had erected between them.

Flora's self-esteem as well as her trust in the external world had been steadily deteriorating from the violent blow which it had received, when she was sixteen years old, from

her envenomed governess, Eliza. Her mother having died
young, and her father absent most of the time, Flora had
been raised entirely by governesses, and Eliza had been for
several years almost the sole adult in Flora's life. Eliza, however, was secretly planning to marry Flora to a disreputable
boy-friend of her own, a Mr. Charles, so as to despoil her
eventually of the fortune which would presumably be set-
tled on her some day by her father, Mr. de Barral, reputed
to be fabulously wealthy. The news came like a thunder-
bolt one day that de Barral had gone bankrupt and had
even been imprisoned for huge financial defalcations. Eliza,
maddened not only by this blow to her ambitions but also
by the fact that she would now never be recompensed for
the sufferings she had undergone in suppressing the jealousy
aroused in her by Charles's philanderings with Flora, turns
upon Flora in a savage outburst and in one moment changes
before Flora's eyes from a trusted adult to a bitter and
venomous harpy. The ages of Eliza and Charles and Flora
are forty, twenty-six, and sixteen. Eliza lets out her venom
on the unsuspecting Flora, the representative in Eliza's eyes
of all the despised employers she had ever had as well as
of the young girls whose youth would be taking away from
her the young men whom a woman of her age could soon
no longer hope to attract.

Flora flees to an acquaintance's house, deaf and dumb
and white faced, and is put to bed in a coma. A few days
later poor relations come to take her into their home, but
there her self-esteem suffers additional blows as her girl-
cousins call her a pauper and the daughter of a convict.
She returns within a year to her acquaintances, the Fynes,
who find for her occasional positions as lady companion or
governess during the next few years, positions which are
soon lost because her employers find Flora too cheerless.

Captain Anthony, Mrs. Fyne's brother, meets Flora at
the Fynes' and falls in love with her. He is many years her

senior and the reason he has never married is that he too has lived nearly all his life with the conviction that he is unlovable. The source of his low self-esteem had been the eminence of his father, who had been a poet of great reputation but a parent indifferent to his apparently untalented children and a domestic tyrant. Captain Anthony understands Flora's self-doubt and despair, because it matches his own, and he feels that the very fact that the world loves neither of them can itself be the basis on which they can love each other. They become engaged to be married, but Mrs. Fyne does not approve of her brother marrying the daughter of a convict and she persuades her husband to convince Anthony that Flora does not love him but has schemed to marry him only in order to provide a home for her father, who is about to be released from the penitentiary.

Captain Anthony, however, decides to go through with the marriage anyway, but he informs Flora that since he is aware of the fact that she cannot love a man as old as he is, he will not exercise his sexual rights over her after their marriage but will devote his life to making her father's last years comfortable. Flora's past history compels her to accept this decision of Anthony's as proof that she is too unattractive to be loved, and her acceptance of his proposal proves to Anthony that although she may have friendly feelings for him she too finds him physically undesirable.

They marry and take de Barral on board ship with them. During the first voyage it becomes apparent that the arrangement is unsuccessful. Flora's father, instead of gratitude, feels hatred for Captain Anthony and regards the ship as a second jail and Captain Anthony as his new jailor. The nervous tension under which the three of them live becomes greater and greater until near the end of the second voyage—when de Barral is caught pouring poison into the Captain's drink. Thereupon Anthony tells Flora that he gives her up, that her father has found an argument against him to which he must accede. Flora is so unnerved by this announcement that she betrays her real feeling for Anthony by involuntarily flying into his arms, crying that she will not let him give her up. De Barral seizes the poisoned drink and commits suicide.

The barriers between Flora and Anthony have now fallen and they proceed to live a happy and normal married life, and one feels that in overcoming those barriers they had not only found each other but had also found their way back to normal relations with whatever social groups they will encounter in the future. Their feeling of estrangement from society, of non-acceptance by others, had been a function of their arrested emotional development towards maturity. Their need for each other had matured them, and normal sexual relations with each other and normal social relations with other people is the natural outcome.

Chapter 33.

THE INN OF THE TWO WITCHES

LIKE AN OUTPOST OF PROGRESS, Conrad's next story, THE INN OF THE TWO WITCHES (1912), deals with the effect which penetration into a foreign country and loss of the familiar supporting social milieu can have upon a man. An awareness of the hostility of society comes gradually to the usual social outcast in Conrad, so that he has time to develop some pattern of neurotic behavior with which to cope with the disorder in his relation to society, but in THE INN OF THE TWO WITCHES the hostility is intense and the person's realization of its existence and of its great intensity comes with one instantaneous blow—and the terrific effect of that blow reveals how dependent a person is, unaware of it though he might generally be, upon the psychological support which a non-hostile social milieu furnishes him. By telescoping into one hour the usual slow and hardening process of social ostracism, Conrad succeeds in sharpening to a deadly needle-point and thereby making extremely vivid the truly malignant character of this social weapon.

The action of the narrative takes place in the year 1810, during the war between England and France. Edgar Byrne, an officer of the British navy, and Tom Corbin, a sailor, have been landed by a British man-of-war on the Spanish coast and Byrne has sent Corbin into an interior mountainous region with despatches to be delivered to Spanish guerillas who are allied to the British. When a local inhabitant of the Spanish coast town warns Edgar that Tom's journey is a dangerous one because the guide he had chosen is a scoundrel, Edgar decides to follow Tom. By nightfall he arrives at an inn and is told that Tom had lodged there the previous night. Edgar decides to stay for the night, but the behavior of the two aged ladies who keep the inn and of the gypsy girl who shows him to his room arouses his suspicions to such an extent that he cannot sleep. He imagines that he hears Tom's voice whispering to him to beware. He searches the room, finds a locked wardrobe, pries open the door and finds Tom there—dead, but without a wound.

Edgar sits up all night trying to discover how Tom died. Suddenly just before dawn he notices the canopy of the bed slowly descending. It sinks noiselessly lower and lower until it settles snugly over the mattress, and Edgar realizes in horror that had he gone to sleep in that bed, he, like Tom, would have been smothered to death.

The experience so unnerves him that the arrival of a troop of soldiers in the inn-yard drives him hysterical and he rushes out to engage the whole troop single-handed. They are his friends, however, the Spanish guerillas. Edgar falls into a delirium and only recovers his senses much later as the guerillas are carrying him back to his ship. They tell him that the two old ladies and the gypsy girl (who had lowered the bed-ceiling with a crank) have been executed.

Like a fissure caused by an earthquake, a deep gulf-like pit had opened at Edgar's very feet, swallowed up his friend Tom, and nearly plunged Edgar himself into the abyss. Although it had happened in a foreign country, the inhabitants thereof were presumably friendly to Edgar's mission there, and the sensation of losing so unexpectedly his sense of security nearly deprives Edgar Byrne of his reason. He had learned with a suddenness of revelation the same kind of knowledge about the external world that the social outcast possesses, and the essential shock of his enlightenment in turn enlightens us as to the full meaning of rejection.

Chapter 34.

BECAUSE OF THE DOLLARS

ONE OF Conrad's recurrent themes has to do with the risks one runs in befriending a social outcast. This was especially evident in A SMILE OF FORTUNE, and it becomes the exclusive sole theme itself in BECAUSE OF THE DOLLARS (1912.) In this story the chief character, Captain Davidson, owes his life, but also the loss of his happiness, represented by his pretty wife and child whom he adored, to his inability to treat a social outcast, a former prostitute by the name of Laughing Anne, with the usual scorn and contempt commonly directed towards persons of that category. The chief ingredient in Captain Davidson's character is simply common decency, that rare thing: an ingrained reluctance to join in a moral condemnation of anyone on conventional grounds.

He had never made any distinction between his manner towards Laughing Anne and his manner towards everyone else during all the years he had known her. After her early years as a prostitute, Laughing Anne had become the mistress of several successive men in the Dutch East Indies, men such as pearl divers casually known to local ship captains such as Davidson. Since the various men with whom she had lived had been acquaintances of Davidson's, he had encountered her many times under differing auspices. Laughing Anne had come to like and respect Davidson because his behavior towards her had never varied or deteriorated in friendliness throughout her many changes of fortune. Some years ago she had disappeared from public sea-port life, but Davidson had recently come across her living with a small trader on a river-bank clearing in the interior near a Malay settlement. She has a six year old son with her, and she tells Davidson she is living with Bamtz, the trader, because he has taken a liking to the boy, the son of another man, and she wishes to raise her son in seclusion and in a family-like environment so that he does not learn about his mother's previous career as a prostitute.

The Malay village where Laughing Anne and Bamtz live is to be Captain Davidson's last stop on a trip he is taking up several Malay rivers to collect all the silver dollars which the Dutch government has called in to be exchanged for new currency. Three thieves have overheard Davidson telling about the dollar-collecting trip and have planned to rob him of his cargo of dollars. They happen to choose Laughing Anne's residence as the place in which to lay in wait for him, and Laughing Anne overhears them plotting to kill her old friend Davidson and rob him of his dollars. When he arrives, Laughing Anne secretly warns him of the plot. When the robbers come on board his ship late at night, Davidson is therefore prepared for them and puts them to rout. The thieves suspect Laughing Anne, dash over to her house and kill her.

Captain Davidson then takes the six year old orphan home with him. He asks his wife to adopt the boy, since they have only one child, a girl. She however (having "a heart about the size of a parched pea") accuses him of being the illegitimate father of the boy and leaves Davidson to go home to England, taking her daughter with her. Davidson places Laughing Anne's boy in an orphanage and becomes a solitary and homeless ship-captain with whitened hair and subdued manner, desolated by the loss of his wife and child. Society is epitomized by his wife, who condemns him to homeless loneliness in punishment for his refusal to cast out from his own life those whom society has seen fit to throw into the discard.

Chapter 35.

THE PLANTER OF MALATA

THE FATE of Adolph Verloc in THE SECRET AGENT, made evident, it will be remembered, that Conrad regarded secretiveness as an anti-social trait, leading one who practices it into ultimate isolation. In THE PLANTER OF MA-LATA (1913) he returns to this theme and gives us Geoffrey Renouard, who runs afoul of the strategic axiom that dissimulation can create present harmony only with persons from whom one is destined to be divided; if used as a device for the purpose of achieving an ultimate harmony with another person, it will ensure the defeat of that purpose and achieve its opposite.

Geoffrey has fallen in love with Felicia Moorsom, who has come from London to the Dutch East Indies in search of her one-time fiance, a Londoner in flight from a charge of embezzlement, later proved unfounded. He had disappeared in that part of the world where Geoffrey lives, and Felicia had persuaded her father to take her to Colonial City so that she can find the man she had promised to marry, inform him of the dropping of the charges against him and of her willingness to go through with the marriage.

She meets Geoffrey in the house of mutual acquaintances. He is struck with her beauty, helps her in her search, but finds that he is falling in love with her himself. He succeeds in locating the missing fiance, only to find that he has been working as a foreman on his, Geoffrey's, own plantation, but that he had died some weeks previously. This news

Geoffrey withholds from Felicia, because he fears that she will immediately return to London and that he will lose her. Felicia and her father accept his invitation that they pay him an extended visit at his plantation on the island of Malata.

After several days Geoffrey takes Felicia to her fiance's grave, tells her about his life and death as a foreman on the ranch, and then proceeds also to tell her that he is himself in love with her and is asking her to marry him. Felicia is so shocked by the news and by Geoffrey's having withheld the truth from her for so long that she recoils in horror from his love-making. His concealment of his love for her, his feigned participation in the search for her fiance, his secrecy and dissimulation has created such a distance between their minds that Geoffrey realizes at last that there is no hope of his ever bridging the gulf he himself has created between them. Felicia goes back to London, and Geoffrey commits suicide. Geoffrey's failure of frankness is the anti-social symbol in this narrative, and it results in his destruction.

Chapter 36.

VICTORY

AXEL HEYST, in VICTORY (1914) reverses the usual role of the social outcast, the man whom society has cast out: Heyst casts out society, withdraws from it and attempts to make of his life a masterpiece of aloofness, willing to live by and for himself alone. He voluntarily and intentionally cultivates and adopts the outcast state, because he desires to enjoy the virtues which he perceives to be essential attributes of the condition of separation from society.

Heyst's failure to succeed in his chosen role means victory for the cohesive principle; his life and death is a victory for the force that draws human beings together into a society and a defeat for that element in human nature which tends to make societies fly apart as though composed of mutually repellant particles, obeying the impulse to separation.

Heyst's father had been a noted philosopher, and by him Heyst had been taught that life itself was an evil, that action of any sort tended to accentuate that evilness, and that nonparticipating and impersonal observation of the spectacle of life should be the sole extent of one's acquiescence in existence.

So Heyst had become a kind of wandering gentleman of leisure, incessantly travelling in the Malay peninsula, one of the few parts of the globe where living was inexpensive enough for him to pay his way on his meagre patrimony.

All went well until one day when Heyst was touched by the sight of a man suffering and in great distress for the lack of a small sum of money with which to pay a fine levied on his ship by an officious port authority. Captain Morrison's ship, his only means of livelihood, was to be sold at auction in order to raise money for the fine, and Heyst was aware of the nefarious legal thievery by means of which Dutch port officials sometimes despoiled an unwary English captain of his ship. Heyst obeyed his impulse to rescue the unfortunate Morrison from his predicament, loaning him the sum needed to pay the fine.

Morrison's gratitude was so overwhelming that it embarrassed Heyst, who rather despised himself for having surrendered to what he considered to be a weakness. Moreover, he found himself helpless to resist Morrison's insistence that he travel on board the ship he had rescued from the auction block until the ship's income had reimbursed Heyst for the loan. Mere repayment of the loan proved to be insufficient to satisfy Morrison, who proceeded to make Heyst his full partner in a coal mining venture on an island in the Archipelago. He deposited Heyst on the island and made him general manager of all operations there.

During one of his trips to England to raise more capital for the mining business, Morrison died. The mining operations ceased soon thereafter and Heyst dismissed all the employees, but he continued to live on the island, he and his Chinese servant its sole inhabitants, except for some natives on the island's far side. He feared that if he resumed his former wandering life he might yield to another compassionate impulse and again get involved beyond his wont in the world's activities.

After the lapse of a year and a half, Heyst signals a passing steamer and goes to the nearest large city where his mail is being held for him. While waiting for the steamer to pick him up again on its return trip, twenty days later, he is assailed nightly by music from the dance orchestra in the hotel's concert hall. It makes him restless and lonely, and he soon forms the habit of spending an hour or two each evening sitting alone at a table listening to the music. One evening he sees one of the girl musicians being abused by the orchestra leader's wife for not having joined the other girl musicians of the orchestra in mingling with the guests during the intermissions, urging them to buy drinks. The girl sees Heyst sitting alone and she joins him at his table.

It is not many days later that Heyst finds himself again impelled to an action inconsistent, like his rescue of Morrison, with his chosen role of non-participating spectator. The girl Lena had spent a good deal of her time at Heyst's table between orchestral performances and Heyst had come nearly every evening to the dance hall. He learns that Lena is an English girl, about twenty years of age, whose life as a travelling musician in an all-girl orchestra is a mere makeshift existence made more dreary by the hostility of the orchestra leader's wife. Moreover, she is being pursued by Schomberg, the owner of the hotel, who waylays her in corridors and becomes every day more importunate and desperate. Heyst foresees her future and the inevitability of her sooner or later becoming the defenseless victim of this or some other predatory Schomberg. Lena communicates her horror of her existence to Heyst so effectively that when they accidentally encounter each other one late night taking solitary walks in the dark garden of the hotel, their physical collision precipitates a kiss which symbolizes his compassionate and protective impulse towards her. She clings to him and he promises to find a way to abduct her from the troupe to which she is contracted.

We next find them living on Heyst's little desert island. Lena is happy in spite of the solitude and the primitive character of her existence there, but she gradually begins to realize that her presence in Heyst's life represents to him not the fulfillment of a need but an apostasy from a lofty ideal of conduct. He feels himself to be no longer the pure observer but to have become one of the objects of observation, vulnerable to the influences of emotion and feelings, and his change of status is very disquieting to him. It becomes her secret ambition to do some deed for Heyst that will make her seem to him a necessary and vital part of himself rather than an embodiment of his failure to make his actions conform to his chosen pattern.

Her opportunity comes with the arrival on their lonely island of three desperadoes in search of plunder. Their visitation had been instigated by Schomberg, whose double motive was to rid his hotel of the illegal gambling carried on by the trio and also to wreak vengeance on Heyst for the abduction of the girl he had chosen for himself. He had convinced the gamblers that Heyst had embezzled a fortune from Morrison and had it hidden in cash on the little island.

Ricardo, the second in command, had hidden from Jones, his senior partner, the fact that a girl lives on the island with Heyst; Jones is a pathological hater of women and this significant trait of his is the key which opens the door to the meaning of the whole novel. Jones equals Heyst in subtlety of culture and breeding; both in their separate ways are at war with society, one actively and one passively; and each is acutely aware of the threat embodied in the female to his resolve to remain a solitary individual, unassimilated by and either warring against or standing apart from the social order. Lena's action, however, in the crisis which now occurs, brings to life the seeds of redemption which exist in Heyst, while Jones the unregenerate remains the mere foil who sets off by contrast the victory for which the Lena-Heyst union stands.

In the battle of wits between the intruders and the island's two inhabitants, Jones pairs off against Heyst and Ricardo against Lena. Ricardo takes care that Jones remains unaware of Lena's existence, pretending that while Jones interrogates Heyst he himself is searching for the hidden plunder. Jones's exhaustion from the rowboat trip to the island from the mainland keeps him confined to a cot in the deserted barracks once used by Morrison's miners, and this enables Ricardo to keep him ignorant of Lena's presence for a period of several days. While Heyst is visiting Jones in the barracks Ricardo steals into Heyst's house and makes a savage sexual attack upon Lena. She, however, to his admiration, successfully fights her way free of him and then pretends to give ear to his proposal that they steal Heyst's money, abandon their gentlemen friends (Heyst and Jones), and run away together. Her motive in listening to him without appearing to take offense is to find some way of protecting Heyst from these evil men; when Heyst returns she helps Ricardo escape through a window and keeps his intrusion a secret from Heyst.

During Heyst's next visit to Jones, Ricardo enters the house again. He is enamoured of Lena and sits at her feet enraptured. He shows her the dagger with which he plans to murder Heyst; she asks to see it; he hands it to her and makes no objection when she hides it in the folds of her dress. At that moment Jones and Heyst suddenly appear in the doorway, Jones having insisted on coming to the house upon being convinced by Heyst that there is no plunder and upon having learned to his astonishment and rage, from Heyst's conversation, of Lena's existence. Jones whips out a revolver and takes a shot at Ricardo but hits and fatally wounds Lena instead. Heyst springs to her side and hears the dying Lena tell him, as she hands him Ricardo's dagger, that she had saved him from death by managing to get possession of and to deliver to him the weapon with which the would-be killer had meant to murder him.

That night Heyst sets fire to his house and follows Lena into death, and by doing so expresses his final conviction that there are things in life worth dying for, a conviction which is contrary to almost the whole cast of his life up to this point. His choosing to die with Lena represents the victory which he has won, with Lena's help, against those elements in his nature that had led him to despise, and isolate himself from, his fellow men.

Heyst is the purest of Conrad's outcasts, the archetype and apotheosis of all outcasts, the man who chooses outcasthood by lofty principle, and by the same token he is also the man in whom is seen most clearly the neurotic root of the withdrawal impulse and the ultimate ineradicability of the need in every man to participate in group formation.

Chapter 37.

THE SHADOW LINE

A MUCH less violent withdrawal from the group and re-entry into it occurs as the central action of Conrad's succeeding story, THE SHADOW LINE (1915). The narrator, who is the central character of this story, had found his life too tame and uneventful as a group-member and had, almost as an act of impulsive caprice, resigned his group-membership and struck out on his own. He had been overcome by an uneasy feeling of being lost in the crowd and by a conviction that in community life he was losing his individuality, that life was slipping away from him.

Although it is a relatively mild attack of revulsion from the group, deriving less from hostility than from boredom, it nevertheless impels him to hazard his career by quitting his job as ship's chief mate in the middle of a voyage at a far-eastern port and booking space as a passenger on a liner bound for England. He had come to a loose end in his life and the response he gave to it took the form of secession from his social group.

Conrad takes up his story at this point and shows us how this man is won back to the group from the very threshold of dereliction. He is approaching that line which, though evanescent as a shadow, divides those who can cross it and reach a state of peace with society from those who by failing to cross it remain all their lives in adolescence, irresolution, and conflict.

Fortunately for the young ex-chief-mate, while he is waiting for the England-bound liner he makes the acquaintance of a retired sea-captain, named Giles, who understands the nature of the crisis in his young friend's life. Captain Giles gently nudges him to apply for the job of captain to a ship whose owners are advertising for someone to take the place on its homeward trip to Europe of the captain who has just died at sea. He is selected for the job and this is his first command.

Had it been an easy one, the trip might not have matured him. But as it turned out, the voyage proved to be so difficult as to test his capacities to their extreme limits. His entire crew falls sick with tropical fever, his ship is becalmed for lack of wind for its sails, the quinine bottles in the medicine chest contain sand instead of medicine, and the previous captain had so terrified the crew with his demented violin-playing that no one believes the winds will come or the fever epidemic abate unless the ship drifts across the meridian where the mad captain had been buried at sea. After agonized weeks the ship does drift across that meridian and the winds do come; the young captain and the cook man the sails and finally get the ship to a port where the sick crew is hospitalized and a new crew signed on.

The reader now feels that with the crossing of that shadow line of longitude where the dead man captain lay buried, the live young captain had also crossed that other shadow line which divides adolescence from maturity, the drifter from the man with a sense of direction, and at the extremes the outlaw from the pacific and responsible member of society.

Chapter 38.

THE WARRIOR'S SOUL

In THE WARRIOR'S SOUL (1916) Conrad veers back to a defense of the individual who, when faced with a conflict between his personal and his social obligations, voluntarily decides to contravene the code of his group and accept ostracism. By means of this story Conrad makes the point that, desirable though it may be for individual conduct to conform to group mores, there are times when an even higher law exacts conduct which sacrifice one's good standing in the group.

Tomassov is a Russian soldier who was faced with the necessity of making a decision of this kind. He had been an attache to the Russian Embassy in Paris when Napoleon declared war on Russia and would have had to languish in French internment for the course of the war had not a friend of his, De Castel, officer in the French army, secretly warned him in time to permit flight over the border before the war broke out. This event places the very grateful Tomassov under obligation to De Castel and the time comes when De Castel calls upon him to pay the debt.

That time comes some months later, during the retreat of Napoleon's army from Russian soil. A nearly frozen French officer, one of the stragglers who had become separated from the fleeing army, comes tottering into a Russian camp one night, attracted by the light and heat of the camp-fire. Tomassov is present and recognizes his friend De Castel. The heat gives the frozen De Castel the cramps and he screams in agony. His death is only a matter of hours, so he demands that Tomassov pay his debt to him by putting a bullet through his benefactor's brain, thus enabling him to avoid suffering through those last few hours of unbearable pain. When Tomassov demurs, since it is a crime to kill a prisoner of war, De Castel calls him a milk-sop.

Goaded by De Castel's agonized demands that he repay his debt to him by doing him this service, Tomassov finally does put De Castel out of his misery. And for having done so he is subsequently courtmartialed and given a dishonourable discharge as punishment for having murdered a prisoner of war. He had accepted a social disgrace in order to fulfill a personal obligation and Conrad does not indicate that Tomassov could have retained his self-respect in any other way.

Chapter 39.

THE TALE

THE READER infers that Tomassov did not regret his decision in later life, but a man who made the opposite decision—the commanding officer in THE TALE (1916) —was haunted ever after by doubts as to the rectitude of the choice he had made. He, like Tamassov, was a military officer on active wartime duty and he also came face to face with the necessity to decide whether to act the way he would have acted had he been a sovereign and autonomous individual or the way it was his duty to act as official representative of the organized group.

If he decides on the latter basis he sends to his death a man of whose innocence he has no proof, whereas if he decides on the former basis he frees a man of whose guilt he has no proof. As an individual he wishes to avoid sentencing a possibly innocent man to death, but as an officer in his country's armed forces he must not risk his nation's safety by permitting a possibly guilty man to go free to do further damage.

The commanding officer is in charge of a British warship which prowls the sea on the lookout for neutral ships suspected of re-fueling enemy submarines. An empty barrel is seen floating on the water, indicating that a submarine had been re-fueled in the vicinity. A great fog comes down and he edges his ship into a nearby cove to anchor. When the fog partially lifts he sees a neutral ship in the entrance to the cove. That ship must have heard the warship edging in during the fog and had not hailed it, thereby indicating that for some guilty reason it did not want to make its own presence known. The commanding officer boards the neutral ship to interview its captain, a Northman, and finds him drunk. He can unearth no evidence to prove that this ship had re-fueled a submarine, but he is certain that the captain and his log-book lie.

So he finally orders the neutral ship to proceed out of the cove, although the fog has not entirely lifted. When the Northman says that he is on a strange coast and doesn't know the way, the commanding officer gives him bearings which will run him on to a ledge of rocks. He thinks that if the Northman is lying, he does know his bearings and will not use the false directions. Then the warship will overtake the ship and capture it.

However, the commanding officer finds out later that the neutral ship had taken his directions and had sunk without survivors.

This event can possibly indicate that the Northman had not lied about re-fueling submarines and that the commanding officer may have been guilty of having sent innocent men to their deaths. He will never know. His decision, as a guardian of his countrymen's safety, to avoid risking a possible increase in the chances of his country's enemies to win the war may have made him personally liable to a self-accusation of having been the agent of injustice and cruelty. He had performed a social duty at the expense of his personal moral certitudes.

Chapter 40.

THE ARROW OF GOLD

BOTH THE ARROW OF GOLD (1918) and YOUTH, and only these two, are unlike all the other Conrad narratives in that they do not have to do in any way with some unpleasantness in the relation between an individual and a group, and they are like each other in that both have to do with an individual's passing from adolescence to adulthood. We may deduce from this that Conrad felt the most pleasurable and satisfying experience in life to be that enjoyed by a youth who for the first time finds himself accepted by grownups as one of themselves; and we may further deduce that Conrad felt adolescence to be not only one form of but also the prototype of all social exclusion. The barriers which adults as a class oppose to youth, however, unlike barriers opposing aspirants to membership in other groups, always fall after a time, and the inevitability of this eventual victory seems to give Conrad deep contentment.

The credentials of adulthood were won by Monsieur George, the young seaman of THE ARROW OF GOLD, when he succeeded in becoming the accepted lover of Rita, a woman slightly older and much more worldly-wise than himself and the queen of a group of admirers who were also older than he. And the diploma, as it were, of adulthood is represented for him by the acceptance, by one of these older admirers of Rita's, of his challenge to a duel. The fighting of the duel is his final graduation out of youth and into manhood.

Monsieur George had completed his first voyage as an

apprentice seaman and is resting in Marseilles. He becomes acquainted with a group of people who are smuggling ammunition from Marseilles by sea into Spain for the partisans of Don Carlos, Pretender to the Spanish throne. Through them he meets Rita, the immensely wealthy young woman who is using her money to buy the ammunition and the ships in which to transport it and to hire the men who man the ships and run the blockade. Monsieur George finds himself so drawn to Rita that he permits her to place him in command of one of her sailing sloops smuggling arms to the Spanish coast.

The other members of the group in which Monsieur George now finds himself are all either much older than he, or higher in the social scale, or both. In comparison with them he is a mere boy, making the first moves in his life's career. In spite of the slightness of her advantage of him in years, Rita has had immensely more worldly experience than Monsieur George. She had been born a Spanish peasant and before she was twenty had become the publicly acknowledged mistress of a man whose social position was of the highest level in Paris, whose wealth was very great, and who had in addition won distinction as a painter. His name was Henry Allegre. He had died and left his entire fortune to Rita, who thereupon becomes the financial backer of Don Carlos, Pretender to the Spanish throne. She does this partly as a personal caprice and partly as a tribute to Allegre, who had been a friend of Don Carlos'.

Rita's choice of Monsieur George to buy, outfit and command a sloop to add to her small fleet already engaged in the ammunition smuggling enterprise places him at one stroke on a level with other much older and experienced men in her retinue. Rita thereby becomes the key which unlocks for him the door standing between youth and manhood, between himself as a young sailor and himself as a responsible adult engaged in a desperate venture.

This, however, proves to be but one stage in his graduated passage to complete adulthood. He begins soon to realize that Rita wants him to become—and that he himself wants to become—her lover. The rapidity with which the maturing effect of this event, his first affair, works on Monsieur George, is enhanced by the fact that two other, older, men already desire Rita and with deadly seriousness. Captain Blunt, a Virginian aristocrat from America and an officer in the Carlist army, means to marry Rita; and Jose Ortega, a Spanish peasant cousin of Rita's, has been murderously lurking just off-stage in Rita's life ever since as a child he had by throwing rocks at her forced from her a promise to marry him.

The growing danger to Monsieur George from these two men, who are becoming maddened with jealousy, incites Rita to spring into action: she carries Monsieur George off with her to the Swiss Alps for a several months' honeymoon in a hideout. But on one of his quick trips to Marseilles to replenish their supply of cash, Monsieur George hears that Captain Blunt is telling everywhere that Rita has become the prey of a young adventurer named Monsieur George. He seeks out Captain Blunt, challenges him to a duel and is shot, but not quite fatally. Rita comes and nurses him back to health, but before he leaves the hospital she leaves him forever—because there are other men who would kill Monsieur George if she should continue to live with him.

He recovers and goes to sea, never forgetting but never seeing her again. During the year which had elapsed since his arrival in Marseilles he had changed from a youth excluded from adult society to a man whom adults accepted as one of themselves. Monsieur George's almost effortlessly successful penetration into the very innermost circle of those engaged in high and desperate enterprise is Conrad's nostalgic tribute to that one short period in every man's life when the barriers fall between the individual as a maturing youth and the group as a society of adults.

Chapter 41.

THE RESCUE

In THE RESCUE (1919), Captain Tom Lingard, like
Kurtz in HEART OF DARKNESS, is torn apart and all
but destroyed by a conflict between two societies both
of which claim him as a member. He feels intense personal
loyalty to groups of people in each of the opposed societies,
and when events beyond his control culminate in a situation
wherein he can save the lives of one group only by sacri-
ficing those of the other, Lingard collapses. Events move on
while Lingard stands paralyzed by indecision: one group of
his friends are killed, and the others are thereby deprived
of his feeling of friendship for them—since the living ones
will always carry, for him, the blood of the dead ones on
their hands.

As Captain Ahab was to Melville, as Don Quixote was
to Cervantes, as Leatherstocking was to Cooper, so was Captain Tom Lingard to Conrad. Tom Lingard embodies Conrad's idea, the basic idea common to all his fiction, more
completely than does any other character and he contains
within himself as elements of his own personality many of
the chief if not most of Conrad's other created characters.
Axel Heyst, for instance, is Lingard become self-conscious,
intellectual, and indecisive by education and inherited
wealth.

Lingard had appeared as a background character and as
an old man in Conrad's first novel, ALMAYER'S FOLLY,
as a chief character and as a not-so-old man in Conrad's

second novel, AN OUTCAST OF THE ISLANDS, and in
RESCUE, Conrad's next to last novel, as the central character and a comparatively young man. The fact that it was
in 1896 that Conrad started writing THE RESCUE, that
he worked at it only occasionally during almost his entire
writing career of twenty-five years, would indicate that he
wanted to save it until he had reached the height of his
powers, so as to be able to make it one of his crowning
achievements as a novelist—which it undoubtedly is.

Captain Tom Lingard owns his own ship, a sailing
freighter, and he earns his living as an independent cargo
carrier in the waters surrounding Indonesia. The dominant
people in the area are the Dutch colonials, who have con-
quered most of the native Malay tribes. Lingard, however,
knows some of the Malay people who had not yielded to
Dutch domination but had retreated to more inaccessible
parts of Borneo and New Guinea, and he likes them better
than he does the Dutch invaders. In fact he likes two of
them so much (Hassim and Immada, brother and sister)
that he risks his life, his livelihood and his ship in their
behalf. It is forbidden by Dutch law to furnish arms and
ammunition to Malays, but Lingard has for two years been
breaking that law by stockpiling a supply of war materiel
in a secret cache for the ultimate use by his two Malay
friends in an attempt to recover their hereditary rulership
over a native province, the succession to which had been
stolen from them by a revolutionary clique. Lingard has
also enlisted the aid of other independent Malay chieftains,
Belarab and Damon, to assist him in restoring Hassim by
force of arms to his position as Rajah over his people, and
he has succeeded in persuading another white friend of the
Malays, Captain Jorgenson, an ex-ship captain married to a
Malay woman, to join in the enterprise as custodian of the
cache of ammunition.

Tom Lingard is a befriender of outcasts, like Heyst in

VICTORY, the captain in A SMILE OF FORTUNE, Kurtz in HEART OF DARKNESS, and the captain in THE SECRET SHARER. Each of these is in some degree "a man without a country," having become more or less detached from the group into which he was born—but without actually reaching an outcast status. These men possess in common the power to survive detachment from their natal groups, and a fascination with the spectacle of those who have less of that power, and an impulse to assist them.

In Hassim and Immada, Lingard sees not only two persons who have been thrust out by their own people but also, since they are Malays, representative symbols of a race which has been thrust out from hegemony over its native lands by the colonial Dutch. The Malay population of Indonesia has become a mass outcast portion of humanity of reason of failure to withstand the military might of the European invader.

Just as Lingard is arriving with his last load of ammunition and just as Belarab's and Damon's warriors are assembling to begin the war on Hassim and Immada's behalf, an English pleasure yacht becomes stranded on a bar very near to the place on the Bornean coast where the ammunition supply is secreted. Lingard is infuriated because if a Dutch gunboat is sent for to float the yacht the gathering of Malay armed forces nearby will come to the attention of the authorities and the ammunition dump will be discovered. If this should happen, Lingard's proteges will have lost the benefit of his two years' labor, and Lingard himself will be in serious trouble with the Dutch authorities.

Lingard boards the stranded yacht and offers to pull it off the reef. Mr. Travers, the owner of the yacht, however, takes an instant dislike to Lingard and loftily rejects his offer of assistance, saying that Dutch gunboats have already been sent for. Hassim and Immada come on board while Lingard is talking with Travers, and they arouse the interest of Travers' wife Edith. She perceives from their dignity and grace of bearing that they are superior specimens of their race and she asks Lingard to tell her about them. Travers however thinks them savage and orders Lingard and the two Malays off the yacht.

Lingard returns that evening and, while Travers and his friend d'Alcacer are taking a walk on the nearby beach, he pours out the story of his life to Edith and explains to her what danger the occupants of the yacht are in from the white-hating Malay warriors encamped nearby. While they talk, Travers and d'Alcacer are captured by Damon's men and imprisoned in a stockade. When Lingard learns later that evening that Damon wishes to execute Travers and d'Alcacer, loot the yacht and massacre its opponents, and is being held in temporary and precarious check only by the urging of the more cautious and peaceful Hassim and Immada, he gets Edith's consent to remove her and the yacht's crew to his own ship for safe-keeping. Edith asks Lingard to get her husband and d'Alcacer back for her.

Lingard goes to Damon and persuades him to release Travers and d'Alcacer into his custody on the condition that they be kept as hostages for the safety of Damon's men, in case, as Damon suspects, the English yacht proves to be a disguised advance scout presaging the arrival of Dutch gunboats. Damon mistrusts everybody because he is a hunted outlaw in the eyes of the Dutch and the presence of the white man's yacht has frightened him. He believes in Lingard's good intentions but feels that even Lingard may not fully realize how crafty and ruse-resourceful the Dutch may be.

During the long negotiations which ensue, prolonged by Belarab's absence on a pilgrimage to his father's tomb, Captain Lingard's chief mate loses his presence of mind and fires on some of Damon's men, killing a few. Damon now begins to mistrust Lingard, and in order to ensure the return of Travers and d'Alcacer to his custody he seizes Lingard's friends, Hassim and Immada.

The issue is now joined. To save the lives of Hassim and Immada, Lingard will have to surrender the lives of Travers and d'Alcacer. There is no way out of this trap for Lingard, because it was one of his own men who had panicked and fired the first shot. When Lingard accepted the terms upon which Travers and d'Alcacer were returned into his custody, he in effect had bound himself by Malay law to pay with a life for a life. He therefore must deliver to Damon the lives of either Travers and d'Alcacer or Hassim and Immada, in payment for the lives of Damon's men, killed by the shots of Lingard's rash and unnerved chief mate. His power to choose is further paralyzed by the fact that he has now fallen in love with Edith Travers and she with him.

The impasse is finally resolved for Lingard by a desperate and despairing act on the part of his lieutenant Jorgenson, guardian of the ammunition which has been stored on an old ship beached in a river. One of Damon's fellow chieftains has come on board that ship, bringing Hassim and Immada with him, and the four of them wait there tensely for Lingard's decision. For a day and a night the tense waiting continues, without any sign from Lingard. Finally at dawn Jorgenson sees that countless Malay canoes, filled with Damon's and his fellow chieftain's warriors, surround his ship. Lingard's inaction will at any moment result in Damon's men seizing the ammunition and massacring all the whites, probably even Lingard and himself as well as the members of Travers' party and the crew of Lingard's ship. In despair, Jorgenson with a lighted cigar in his mouth jumps down into the hold of the ship where the ammunition is stored, thus causing it to explode and kill everybody on board and around the ship.

This event so appals everyone that the whites are permitted to go back to their ships in peace. Lingard has one last interview with Edith in which he tells her that she had taken his strength away and deprived him of the power to help his friends. He turns his back on her and sails north in his ship while Edith returns to her husband—whose ship sails south.

Lingard is again a lone individual, with all ties severed which had bound him to two different groups—which in turn represented two different civilizations. Edith Travers represented the best in one civilization and Hassim and Immada the best in the other. But these two points of contact for Lingard with their respective social groupings were themselves without power among their own people and therefore could not, even with Lingard's help, restrain their respective groups from those hostile acts towards each other which finally brought down ruin on everybody. Furthermore, it was the hostile act on the part of Lingard's own chief mate, whose fear and suspicion of the Malays overpowered him, that precipitated the final disastrous chain of events.

So in fact the true villain of the novel, the one factor which defeated Lingard's attempts to establish and maintain an abiding relation with both groups, was the irrational hostility of one racial group for another. Lingard lost control over the course of events because inter-group hostility became too strong for him.

Captain Lingard had made a superhuman effort, exerting all his strength, to break out of the solitude and isolation of his own independent existence, and his effort to do so had taken the form of backing against their destiny persons almost as solitary and isolated as himself. His failure was due, ultimately, to the misdeed of the Dutch in having enforced upon the Indonesian people an outcast status. Mr. Travers' contempt, and Lingard's chief mate's fear, of people whom they deemed their racial inferiors, clashing with Damon's

hatred of the race which had attempted and nearly succeeded in exterminating his own, had defeated Lingard's
hopes of forming personal social ties which cut across these
factitious racial barriers. Conrad's sympathy, as shown in
THE RESCUE, is clearly with those who, by "going native"
like Jorgenson, had cast their lot by choice on the side of
the outcasts.

Chapter 42.

THE ROVER

IN HIS last novel, THE ROVER (1922), Conrad tells the
story of Jean Peyrol, a renegade and near-outlaw who in
his old age secretly returns incognito to his native land and
the scenes of his boyhood and there performs a great and
heroic deed—without any hope of reward, for he voluntarily
sacrifices his life in the performance of this deed—which enables his country to win one round in its war with a great
and powerful enemy. The hunted outcast therefore turns
out to be a more serviceable member of his natal group than
the vast majority of its conforming members.

After a fifty year absence from his native country, France,
from which he had fled as a boy to avoid military service,
Jean Peyrol returns home to the farm near Toulon on which
he had been born son to a servant-girl. He had spent the
fifty years in the East Indies as a roustabout sailor, sometimes it is rumored as a member of "The Brotherhood Of
The Coast," pirates preying on China Sea shipping. He tells
the people who now live on the farm that he had once as
a boy lived there as a farmhand, persuades them to rent
him a room in the farmhouse, and settles down to live the
last years of his life in the same physical surroundings as
those he had first become acquainted with as an infant. In
his vest are sewed sixty or seventy thousand francs in gold
pieces, which we are given to understand are loot acquired
during his lawless life in the Far East.

The time is about 1800 and the proprietor of the farm,

Scevola Bron, had been one of the fanatic zealots of the French Revolution and had acquired the property by having its owners guillotined for harboring anti-revolutionary refugees. Scevola's title to respectability is therefore sounder than Jean Peyroll's only by virtue of the fact that political upheavals had come to rest with the law-making power in the hands of the revolutionaries instead of in those of the old regime. Scevola, however, means to further legitimize his claim to the farm by marrying the original owner's daughter, Arlette, who is now twenty years of age and still lives on the farm along with her Aunt Catherine, sister of Arlette's father.

Arlette however hates and fears Scevola, and falls in love with Lieutenant Real, whom Napoleon has sent into the neighborhood to watch the movements of Lord Nelson's English fleet which is blockading the French coast. Lieutenant Real also loves Arlette; but he is unable to court her, because he has been ordered by Napoleon to let himself be captured by the enemy while carrying secret despatches which, being false, will lure the British fleet on a wild-goose chase to another part of the Mediterranean.

Jean Peyrol succeeds in finding out what Lieutenant Real's secret mission is, whereupon there slowly matures in his mind a determination to supplant Lieutenant Real in the carrying out of the mission. A crescendo of motives impel him to this decision: (1) his desire to rescue Arlette from Scevola's designs upon her, (2) his desire to remove the obstacle which prevents the union of Arlette and Lieutenant Real, and (3) above all his desire to perform some act which will have the effect of re-uniting him, even if only in death, with the group or society to which he has been for a lifetime, at least outwardly, renegade.

A ruse enables Peyrol, while Lieutenant Real is saying goodby to Arlette, to slip out to sea at the helm of the small sailboat on which the secret and misleading despatches are hidden. Ostensibly a mere fishing boat, the small craft is handled by Peyrol, who is a consummate sailor, in such a way as intentionally, but as if without intention, so as to be more convincing, to arouse the suspicions of the British cruiser hovering nearby. When the cruiser gives chase, Peyrol makes every effort to give the appearance of attempting to escape. He carries these efforts to such lengths that the cruiser finally begins firing shots at the sailboat. Even then Peyrol refuses to surrender. More shots not only disable the sailboat but also kill Peyrol—as well as Scevola who had been, without Peyrol's being aware of it, hidden on the boat.

The captain of the cruiser discovers the despatches and delivers them to Lord Nelson, who, finding that they indicate a movement of the French Navy to Egypt and thinking them genuine, since a man had given his life to protect them, thanks the cruiser captain for the valuable capture. In admiration for his seamanship and refusal to surrender, the British give Peyrol an honorable burial by placing his body on the sailboat, fastening a French flag to the mast of the little craft and then sinking it by gunfire, as though it were a salute.

Lieutenant Real and Arlette marry—and revere the memory of Jean Peyrol. They find his vest, lined with gold-pieces, at the bottom of a well. Real suspects them to be pirate-loot, but he does not tell Arlette that Peyrol had been a pirate: he merely tells her that Peyrol had been a good Frenchman. By means of his last great deed and the manner of his death, Jean Peyrol had found a way to reconcile himself with the human community to which his lifetime relation had been that of renegade, exile, and outcast.

CONCLUSION

CONRAD WAS born into a family of revolutionary Polish patriots and at a time when Czarist Russian oppression of the subject Polish nation was most galling. When Conrad was five years old his father was arrested by the Russian police for having taken part in a Polish rebellion and was deported to northeast Russia, sentenced to live there under police supervision, an exile from his native land. His wife and young son accompanied him into exile.

For three years, from his fifth through his eighth year, the boy Conrad lived in what today we call a "concentration camp." His mother died there, unable to endure the hardship. The eight year old boy was thereupon separated from his father, sent back to Poland, and placed in the household of an uncle for upbringing.

Five years later, when Conrad was thirteen years old, his father was sent home to die, his health completely shattered. He died within a year of his return.

Three years later, at the age of seventeen, Conrad left Poland and never resided there again, scarcely ever even visiting it.

The following words occur in a book (SOME REMINISCENCES) which he wrote many years later (1912): "Having broken away from my origins under a storm of blame from every quarter which had the merest shadow of right to voice an opinion, removed by great distances from such natural affections as were still left to me, and even estranged, in a measure, from them by the totally unintelligible character of the life which had seduced me so mysteriously from my allegiance . . ."

In the light of these facts about Conrad's violently patriotic family, his early formative years, and his voluntary depatriation—is it any wonder that the novels and short stories written by a man with such a background should be obsessed by the specter of the outcast, the rebel, the nonconformist, and by the themes of guilt and rejection of guilt?

Instead of carrying on his father's fight for Polish independence, a fight in which both his father and his mother had lost their lives, Conrad had turned his back on his countrymen and run away to sea. That deed, and the emotions and perceptions it gave rise to, was the genesis of, and furnished the themes for, the forty-two pieces of fiction which Conrad subsequently wrote—many of which are now numbered among the acknowledged masterpieces of English literature.

Conrad was a non-conformist not only to the revolutionary traditions of his father's family but also to the conciliatory traditions of his mother's people, who were more inclined to come to terms with the Russian conqueror. Unwilling either to live peaceably under the rule of his parents' murderers or to take part in recurrent and futile Polish rebellions, he chose instead to shake the dust of Poland from his feet, to break all ties with the people among whom he had been born and raised, and to take up the life of a sailor on all the oceans of the earth. It was at the age of seventeen that Conrad separated from his natal group; and he did so, moreover, as he says, "under a storm of blame from every quarter," accused of having been "seduced" from his "allegiance." His life as a separate individual, "estranged" from his own people, began under clouds of disapproval so dark that they started in him a lifetime of meditation on the subject of non-conformity.

Sometime during the following decade, while working as

a seaman on some sailing freighter, Conrad wrote his first story. Its theme of discrepancy between appearance and reality, wherein circumstances unjustly conspire to exclude a man from membership in a group to which he had every valid right to belong, translates so clearly into Conrad's personal situation relative to his countrymen back home in Poland as to render the story a fable contrived to fit his personal predicament. That is, no doubt, why Conrad did not publish THE BLACK MATE until near the end of his life. The attitude of the ship-captains to the whitened hair of the "black" mate corresponds of course to that of his Polish compatriots to Conrad's act of abandoning the problem of Polish-Russ relations: the deduction naturally being that the attitude of the latter group was based, as was that of the former, on a misinterpretation of facts and motives.

Winston Bunter's prematurely gray hair is his mark of non-conformity, which furnishes the basis for the discrimination against him. The resort to camouflage is the first weapon that Conrad hands to Winston Bunter, and when that fails he teaches him the trick of making the mark of non-conformity seem to signify something highly esteemed, however irrationally, by those in authority—instead not only of what it really signifies but also instead of what it had been supposed to signify by those who condemned it.

Duplicity is used to put things to rights again, in THE BLACK MATE. The non-conformist is restored to his place in society; he is shown to be in truth uninjurious to the society which had been rejecting him; and society is shown first to have been duped by its own misconceptions (to its own injury) and then to have been duped by the non-conformist, to its own (as well as his) benefit.

This was but Conrad's first light skirmish with his theme, and its main function was, by probing, to make contact with his enemy, his subject, his engrossing preoccupation. With this story he located the area of his obsessive interest, made an initial definition of its nature, and began the long process of self-analysis which the traumas of his boyhood and early youth had made necessary to him.

In his second work, his first published novel, AL-MAYER'S FOLLY, Conrad traced a man's progressive degeneration and ultimate defeat to his desire to justify his life as an emigrant in the eyes of those who comprised his home country's society—and it was as though Conrad were warning himself not to do as Almayer did. Almayer's belated want to conform with the mores of the society from which he had sprung interfered with his conformity to the society in which he and his half-breed daughter live. He came to ruin because he was a conformist by nature but a non-conformist in behavior—and the reef which wrecked him is one that Conrad had had to navigate in his own life.

After meeting with and disposing of the temptation to spend a lifetime in the endeavor to persuade the people back home to understand and accept his act of separating himself from them and their problems, Conrad passed on in his next novel, THE OUTCAST OF THE ISLANDS, to the next temptation which lies in wait for the non-conformist: that of thinking it possible and desirable to live apart from and independent of any social group whatever. In Willems Conrad pictures for us a man who is congenitally unable to comprehend the very concept of the group as an entity in itself. Apparently Conrad's experience with the first social group in his life, the one in Poland where he had lived as a youth, had conditioned him to some extent against all social groups and he had therefore been subsequently forced to face the temptation of choosing to live a completely individualistic life, involved as little as possible in the life of any group. He however taught himself the dangers of following such a choice by telling the sorry story of Willems' un-social career.

In THE NIGGER OF THE NARCISSUS Conrad presented—and carried to its logical conclusion—yet another way to live with the non-conformist elements in one's nature. That way is to use one's non-conformity as a disruptive and disintegrative weapon against the group in the interest of self-aggrandisement. James Wait's specific way of doing this was to impersonate the non-conformist character at a time strategically chosen to force the hand of authority into punishing him so publicly as to excite the latent hostility which many group members feel against those dominant over them. Self-pity lies at the root of this hostility, self-pity in the guise of pity for the downtrodden—and it was this root that Wait tapped. He exploited the resource available to all non-conformists of goading those in authority over the group into exacting a penalty of them so severe as to win for the penalized ones the sympathy and support of the majority, thus deflecting the social disapproval away from themselves and towards the group leaders. But Conrad found, through Wait, that to linger in this way-station among the various emotional states induced in one by the non-conformist role is merely to invite self-destruction and that therefore one must journey on.

In THE IDIOTS non-conformity appears as an inability to bear a child that is not an idiot. Jean and Suzan Bacadou are involuntary and unwilling and self-condemned non-conformists, but they nevertheless suffer even more severely than do those whom society punishes for having by choice dared to deviate.

Murder and suicide end the lives not only of Jean and Suzan in THE IDIOTS but also of Kayerts and Carlier in the succeeding story, THE OUTPOST OF PROGRESS, and in both cases the root cause of the disaster is a feeling of shame and disgrace for not meriting social approval. For permitting their minds to dwell on the pain of having lost their right to the esteem of their countrymen, these four people lost their lives. Conrad therefore seems to be saying that since this is the price some people are willing to pay for failure to conform to the expectations of the social group to which they belong, it can readily be seen what tremendous weights of pressure must be endured by anyone (such as himself) who had incurred the displeasure of his fellowmen.

With Karain, in KARAIN: A MEMORY, Conrad looks wistfully and nostalgically at the resource which was once available to men, when civilization was in its infancy, of finding in amulets and charms the power to hold at bay the dread menace of guilt-feelings.

With Alvan Hervey, in THE RETURN, and Arsat, in THE LAGOON, Conrad reminds himself that after all situations do occur in human living wherein certain essential values cannot possibly be preserved or attained except by a course of action which involves giving affront to one's social group. In these instances the values thus secured are greater than those lost by severance from the group.

And in YOUTH, Conrad perceives with Marlowe that in moving out of boyhood and into manhood the gain of achieved membership in the society of adults is greater than the loss of relinquished membership in the society of adolescents.

HEART OF DARKNESS marks Conrad's first peak of emancipation from neurotic involvement in the coils of guilt which had been winding about him, and with which he had been wrestling like Laocoon, ever since he had shaken the dust of revolutionary Poland from his feet. In Kurtz he had created an individual almost great enough to encompass and transcend two great mass groups: European civilized society and the black hordes of barbarous Africa. For the first time in Conrad, the individual no longer stands at bay, facing society like a hunted animal, but turns and takes the initiative, actively judges and becomes in a degree a creative shaper of the social group. Kurtz is a non-conformist so powerful that he makes whole societies swerve, even though ever so slightly, from their orbits. For Marlowe, who was sensitive and intelligent enough to feel the full impact of Kurtz's nobility and power, the dicta of organized social orders will never again be absolute and unquestioned. And as for Conrad himself, we feel when reading HEART OF DARKNESS that this story was his personal declaration of independence from that centripetal force in society which tends to make conformists of us all.

II.

LORD JIM's jump from the boat *Patna* is curiously reminiscent of Joseph Conrad's desertion of his Polish compatriots as a young man of seventeen. The novel LORD JIM is Conrad's great act of tacit contrition, conceived by him during one of those periods when a shake of the kaleidoscope had made the elements of his past life fall into such a pattern as to make it seem even to him that his departure from Poland had been a breach of good conduct. Lord Jim's failure to prove the judges of the Official Inquiry wrong about him stands for Conrad's failure to reverse the opinions of those who had blown "a storm of blame from every quarter" upon him when he had "broken away from his origins." Both Conrad's Poland and Lord Jim's boat *Patna* had survived after all, in spite of the derelict despair of their respective custodians. And Lord Jim's failure to deal realistically with the outlaw Brown is Conrad's warning to himself and others that the man of imagination is ipso facto unfit for any post of responsibility in the public world of social and political structures.

Such men as Captain MacWhirr, in TYPHOON, however, being devoid of imagination, are the ones who by that very fact are eminently fitted to deal adequately with the kinds of decisions which lie waiting in the path of those who choose to live in, and even accept posts of responsibility in, the world of social and political structures.

With Lord Jim and Captain MacWhirr, Conrad is saying again what he said with Winston Bunter: the thing to do with a blemish is to transform it into a badge of honor, or in other words many men of imagination are laden with guilt and failure while other slow-thinking dolts go through life without making an error.

The somewhat neurotic attitudes in Conrad himself, as betrayed by these two stories, are carried to a further extreme in AMY FOSTER. The parallelism between Yanko Gooral, the Carpathian peasant shipwrecked on the coast of England, and Joseph Conrad, the Polish refugee trying to get a foothold in English literary circles, is obvious. This, like so many of Conrad's stories, repeats, as though in a nightmare, aspects of Conrad's personal life. The vividness with which Conrad communicates to us Yanko's sense of being lost and forlorn in a foreign land far from home makes us feel certain that at least at times and in certain moods Conrad himself must have felt that way in the England to which he had transplanted himself.

In FALK: A REMINISCENCE, Conrad's feeling of guilt at having abandoned his Polish compatriots to their fate at the hands of the Russians becomes Falk's guilt at having eaten the flesh of his shipmates when the broken ship on which he works, drifting rudderless out of the paths of shipping until the food is gone, reduces its crew to the last extremity. Conrad's jump out of Poland is the equivalent of Falk's eating of human flesh, and both men are haunted by a feeling of estrangement from humankind until they can publicly relate their history, explain how necessary and unavoidable their deeds were, and receive society's absolution.

TOMORROW is concerned with one of the injurious consequences of a too solitary and socially restricted life:

the unhealthy stimulus which such a life provides for the imagination. Deprived by her invalid father of normal social relations, Bessie Carvil fell into the trap of permitting her imagination to fill the void which non-participation in any group-life had inflicted upon her. In addition to the pernicious effects of isolation upon the individual, the story TOMORROW also deals with discord in the parent-child relationship. Harry Hagberg, like Conrad himself, had run away to sea while yet a boy, thereby incurring the displeasure of his father just as Conrad had incurred the displeasure of his parents' surviving relatives. And Bessie Carvil had been psychologically injured by her tyrannical and invalid father, just as Conrad had been injured by his father's carelessness in engaging in political activities so dangerous as to bring down upon himself exile and early death.

In THE END OF THE TETHER, the issue at stake is Captain Whalley's success or failure in avoiding a state of non-conformity to the standards of either one of two conflicting groups: his family and his profession. This was also the issue at stake in Conrad's personal life, and the fact that in Captain Whalley's case Conrad makes a morally blameless circumstance, the physical defect of failing eyesight, the cause for the existence of the conflict of interest between the two groups indicates that Conrad is searching in this story for a formula which will lift the weight of guilt off his own personal shoulders.

The novel NOSTROMO also performs this service for Conrad, but more directly and on a grander scale. The historical evolution of Costaguana is related in such a way as to show how futile political revolts in the interests of freedom must necessarily be until such time as powerful economic and material interests also need that same freedom which is desired by the liberals for ideational and humanitarian reasons only. NOSTROMO is Conrad's painstakingly elaborated explanation for his defection from the ranks of

the Polish revolutionary patriots. By means of this novel
Conrad is saying that the Poles who wanted to fight for independence from Russia did not have the support of any
powerful material interests within Poland itself and were
therefore strengthless. It was Conrad's opinion that belief in
the nineteenth century liberal and humanitarian faith that
abstract ideals of progress and justice possessed power had
killed his father and mother and made him, their son, an
outcast from his native land. NOSTROMO is Conrad's attack upon the Victorian respectable pretense that the center
of strength lay in abstract ideals rather than in economic
forces.

What has all this to do with conformity? Simply this:
that Conrad is maintaining by means of this novel that his
personal non-conformity to the ideals of the family and
national group into which he had been born was based on
a deeper sense of history than were the loyalties which he
had rejected. Therefore it was his need to conform to a
deeper truth that had forced him into non-conformity with
the shallower one.

The two succeeding stories, THE INFORMER and
THE SECRET AGENT, tell what happened to two men
who were mere pretenders at conformity. By means of these
two stories Conrad is saying that to evade the penalties of
non-conformity by feigning a conformity which one does
not feel and by hiding one's true identity is to incur even
worse sufferings. In order to remove from his two instances
of this form of behavior all taint of cowardice and to insert
in its place the more laudable emotion of courage in the
defense of the established order, Conrad makes his characters
police spies who have, as a part of their jobs, become members of subversive anarchist groups. The suffering which
they are forced to endure as a direct consequence of this
dishonesty consists of eventually losing the power to com-
munciate even with those persons to whom their hearts

draw them. These stories say to those people who had blamed Conrad for leaving Poland that if he had done as they wished him to do he would have lost his basic honesty and invited the same sort of penalty as Comrade Sevrin and Adolf Verloc brought down upon themselves.

The novelette named THE DUEL refines and sharpens Conrad's definition of his attitude to conformity and non-conformity in that by this story he refutes the supposition that his refusal to conform to the society in which he found himself as a youth was due to a predisposition on his part to non-conformity for non-conformity's sake. Rebel though he was against the role of Polish revolutionary which his family inheritance had nearly thrust upon him, he makes it plain by mean of THE DUEL that in reality he is on the other hand so predisposed by nature in favor of conformity as to be inclined, with d'Hubert, to refrain at almost any cost from giving offense even to obsolete and antiquated social customs and those who practise them.

The theme of predilection for conformity is even more strongly stated in GASPAR RUIZ than it is in THE DUEL. By a mere misadventure Gaspar is thrown out by a group which had not long before enrolled him as a member by conscription and his entire subsequent life is spent in fierce struggling to regain acceptance by that group. His attempts to force the group to let him conform take on such ferocious proportions as to make of him a non-conformist raised to the nth degree, a specimen of non-conformism incarnate. The violence however of his aggression against the group which had cast him out directly expresses the strength of his desire to be permitted to become a conforming member of that group. Thus Conrad removes from the realm of possibilities any conjecture that he himself possesses any personal bias in favor of rebelliousness per se.

In IL CONDE society is pictured as even more of an evil aggressor against the individual than it is in GASPAR

RUIZ. Neither the old count nor Gaspar Ruiz had given society just cause for its perverse malice towards them. Both stories place on society the entire blame for the estrangement between the individual and the social group. Conrad is therefore in these stories hurling back at his former associates in Poland that "storm of blame" which they had directed at him when he "broke away from his origins." THE BRUTE marks the very nadir of Conrad's desolate feeling of alienation from his environment. In this story the very stuff of the universe seems to be animated by a hostile feeling towards the individual, just as organized human societies had been in the two preceding stories. And in all three cases this hostility is gratuitous and unmerited, an evil and unwarranted aggression against a guiltless victim. Conrad is here totally committed on the side of the solitary individual, to the destruction of whom the total environment is conceived of as being dedicated.

With AN ANARCHIST Conrad makes the first move in his counterattack against the feeling of desolation pervading the group of stories ending with THE BRUTE. The point made by Crocodile Paul is that, even though an evil society should drive one into isolation and solitude, all is not lost when one loses membership in his group. A solitary life is better than no life at all and it is after all possible to live one's life in anonymity and seclusion and to eke out even in that condition some modicum of happiness.

UNDER WESTERN EYES tells somewhat the same story as did THE INFORMER and THE SECRET AGENT, except that Razumov finally saves his life by throwing off the pretense of conformity which he had been persuaded to adopt, while Comrade Sevrin and Adolf Verloc had lost theirs by not doing so. Haldin, like Conrad's father, had sacrificed his life in assailing Russian despotism, and Razumov, like Conrad himself, had had to repel the at-

tempt to force upon him one or more roles tailored for him
by the actions of others. Two opposed political groups had
tried with partial success to impose their characteristic conformities upon Razumov, but he had found them both to
be alien to the pattern which his life had begun to form.
His attempts to conform first to Haldin's expectations about
him and then to Councillor Mikulin's, the latter entailing
an attempt at playing the role of wolf-in-sheep's-clothing,
wrenched him into a situation so incongruous with the
scholarly life he had intended to live that only violent
revolt restored him to the conformities which he deemed
more congenial to the bent of his nature.

When he wrote THE SECRET SHARER Conrad had
recovered somewhat from the depressed state in which, as
in IL CONDE, THE BRUTE, and THE ANARCHIST, he
had seen life as ferocious and sinister. The thought that
sheep in wolf's clothing, such as the captain encountered by
Leggatt in THE SECRET SHARER, do exist marks the
entrance at this time of a more encouraged note into Conrad's emotional tone. All is not lost if it is possible for a
fugitive from "justice," an outcast, to find an officer of the
law, an enforcer of conformity, who will help him to escape
from his pursuers and thus furnish at least token evidence of
fissures in the apparently solid ranks opposed by society to
the deviant individual. Conrad is saying by means of this
story that the Leggatts of this world, the individuals who
have in one way or another become estranged from their
social group, may take heart from the fact that even among
the wielders of power in the name of the group there are
occasional individuals who secretly sympathize with, and
protect, the estranged ones, the Ishmaelites.

Like THE SECRET SHARER, A SMILE OF FOR-
TUNE is written not from Conrad's usual point of view,
that of the outcast looking with fear at society, but from
that of the secure and eminent member of society looking

with sympathy and fellow-feeling at the outcast. The difference between Alice Jacobus and Leggatt is that Alice has become a confirmed Ishmaelite who does not want to be rescued while Leggatt gives instant response to the captain's invitation to board his ship. Conrad's personal history had made him, he felt, so over-sensitive and over-imaginative and over-responsive to distress calls as to invent them when they did not exist. This special awareness of the pitfalls of gullibility seems to have been unusually deep-seated in Conrad, because evidences of it occur frequently in his fiction. Captain Lingard, for instance, once was bitten by a sick dog which he had found on the beach and carried in his arms to his ship with the intention of nursing it back to health. His most lucrative trading post, also, was reduced to bankruptcy by an act of Willems', the ne'er-do-well whom he had rescued several times from collapse and extinction. Captain Davidson loses his adored wife and child when he takes pity on and brings home the orphan child of the ex-prostitute, Laughing Anne. And Axel Heyst's troubles all result from his inability to refrain from attempting to shore up the collapsing careers of Captain Morrison and Lena.

In A SMILE OF FORTUNE, however, the captain wins through to the solid ground on the far side of the quicksands of sentimentality and successfully resists the temptations to sponsor Alice Jacobus in the teeth of the society which had shunned her. Conrad seems to be describing the almost fatal attraction which the outcast and the non-conformist have for him, and to be making the point that to take any action in excess of a mere refusal to shun is a quixotic mistake.

The fate of Jasper Allen, however, in FREYA OF THE SEVEN ISLES, is presented by Conrad in such a way as to make the tale almost a clarion call to arms against constituted authority. Conrad's account of Lieutenant Heemskirk's perversion of his power as an officer of the law to destroy a personal rival seems calculated to add fuel to the fires of a non-conformist's rage against officialdom. Heemskirk thought that he had successfully eluded detection and penalty for his crime; but he was mistaken, because he now stands exposed and pilloried as an object of scorn and contempt in the eyes of millions of people, the past, present, and future readers of Conrad's FREYA OF THE SEVEN ISLES. And, for many generations to come, haters of law and order will continue to find comfort and justification for their anti-social animus in the spectacle of the despicable Heemskirk seated in the saddle of power.

THE PARTNER also tells the story of a man who commits a crime and, escaping detection, remains a member of society in good standing. Cloete, however, in addition to deserving but avoiding social condemnation for deeds evil and hidden like Heemskirk's, also commits acts as an individual which are injurious to the group, the partnership, of which he is an integral member. In his first aspect, Cloete deserves to suffer but succeeds in escaping the penalties which social outcasts often are made to suffer undeservedly, and in his second aspect he exemplifies one of the ways in which nonconformity itself can be an evil: i.e. when an individual uses the power accruing to him by reason of his group membership to commit acts of which the group disapproves.

In PRINCE ROMAN Conrad tells the story of a man whom Conrad himself might have been had he followed rather than spurned the advice of those friends of his who had blown a "storm of blame" upon him when he "broke away from his origins." The story does not indicate a regret on Conrad's part for having rejected his friends' advice, but it does present sympathetically and with understanding the path they had wished him to follow. By writing this imaginative life which he narrowly missed living in reality, Con-

rad finally washed away the remaining traces of the bitterness which resentment of his friends' "storm of blame" must
have given birth to in him.

The novel CHANCE, however, furnishes at least indirect
evidence that Conrad knew his personal malaise to have
originated long previous to his stormy departure from Poland
at the age of seventeen. He must have finally traced the
source of his fascination with the problem of the non-conformist and the social outcast back to his early awakening
between the ages of five and eight to the fact that he was
the child of proscribed parents, living in enforced exile
far from home and under the surveillance of political police. One may deduce that Conrad had arrived at this stage
of self-knowledge from the fact that the novel CHANCE,
though written in pre-Freud times, tells the story of a neu-
rosis, from its inception in early childhood experiences,
through its growth during adolescence and continuance during early adulthood, to its final cure by means of an involuntary and emotionally explosive affirmation, at a moment
of heightened crisis in feeling, of suppressed desires. The
lives of both Captain Anthony and Flora de Barral had been
deformed by the father influence, just as Conrad's had been,
and the psychological homelessness of Flora's adolescence as
well as the lofty esteem which certain circles had felt for
Anthony's father have their counterparts in Conrad's personal life. The conclusion is therefore inescapable that this
novel too was an act of self-revelation on Conrad's part and
that it probed even deeper into his roots than the stories
which preceded it.

The neurotic feeling of insecurity which is the theme
of CHANCE is also the dominant note struck in THE INN
OF THE TWO WITCHES. In the latter story the feeling
is raised to the pitch of terror and temporary madness and
is based on a single event in the life of an adult individual,
but the two stories have a common concern with the loss

of rapprochement between individuals and their human environments.

And in BECAUSE OF THE DOLLARS Conrad goes on to show how deep is the cleavage between the type of person such as Captain Davidson who chooses to include the insecure ones among those for whom he has group feeling and the type, such as Mrs. Davidson, who chooses to cast them further adrift.

In THE PLANTER OF MALATA Conrad represents lack of candor as a strategic blunder in a personal relation, but in the context of his other fiction it seems clear that his antagonism to secretiveness derives ultimately from a feeling on his part that it is a form of anti-social individualism, a spot of hidden decay which is more damaging both to the indvidual and to the group than open opposition and non-conformity.

With the novel VICTORY Conrad finally comes to the writing of his great saga of conversion from non-conformity to conformity, from withdrawal to participation, from father-worship to love of a mate. The cure in CHANCE and the conversion in VICTORY arrive as the end event of a chain which in each case begins with an act of alliance between two persons both of whom are more or less at odds with society. This act of alliance is in essence a first step in the formation of a new social group and in a retreat from extreme independent individualism. The movement in both of these novels is on the part of the individual and it is in the direction of normalized social relations and a rapprochement of some sort with society in the aggregate. And in both novels the non-conforming inclinations of each of the principal characters are traced to an unhappy childhood and to the influence of a blameworthy father. Reconciliation with society comes about only with a final release from parental domination.

THE SHADOW LINE also tells the story of a man who

made his peace with society, after having broken it during an extended mood of neurotic aberration. In this case Conrad does not trace the outbreak to childhood malformation or parental malfeasance but seems to imply that it is a shadow line that everyone crosses, some with more difficulty than others, as one of the last acts in the achievement of adulthood and emotional maturity. The inference seems to be that conformity comes very hard to some individuals, but that since nonconformity is the equivalent of adolescence the ordeal of shedding it is escaped only by those who continue to be children all their lives.

The situation and events presented in THE WARRIOR'S SOUL, on the other hand, serve as a reminder that instances do occur wherein non-conformity to one prescribed code of conduct is required of a person who feels constrained to obey the mandate of another, conflicting, and in his opinion superior code. If, as in this case, the code which is conformed to possessses few but superior adherents while the code which is contravened is that of a large and powerful social group, the choice made—even though it resulted in social ostracism—is an adult and mature one rather than adolescent.

In THE TALE the opposite choice is made: that of conforming to the coded requirements of the larger social group instead of to those of a more personal and sensitive ethics. The consequence to the man who made this choice is that although he maintains his good standing in the social group he finds that he has burdened himself with depressive feelings of private guilt. The nonconformist of THE WARRIOR'S SOUL is in the end happier than the conformist of THE TALE—and deservedly so.

The theme of youth as an archetype of the outsider, the prototype of the kept out if not the cast out, as set forth in THE ARROW OF GOLD, is clearly corollary to the conception as seen in VICTORY and THE SHADOW

LINE of non-conformity as a form of adolscence. The emphasis in the former is upon youth's victory in eventually establishing itself securely within the formerly excluding walls of adult society, and in the latter upon adult society's victory in eventually prevailing upon the adolescent to abandon his non-conformity; but in both cases the social group is presented as being a natural and desirable home for the individual.

THE RESCUE, however, presents Conrad's greatest created character, Captain Tom Lingard, as a perpetually homeless man, and more mature even as a perennial adolescent than any mere conformer. Friend of all homeless people, and welcome in many homes but at home in none, Captain Lingard penetrates so deeply into so many societies and so many individual lives and consequently possesses so many sides as a person that he finally seems to be not only a single-handed rival of whole social groups but even to constitute within himself alone the equivalent of a whole social group. He is at once a non-conformist to, and a supporter of conformity to, all societies; an enemy to all conflict between societies and an advocate who pleads the cause of the outcast at the bar of society. In fact, Lingard is Conrad, both the elemental and ultimate man that Conrad contained within himself.

With THE RESCUE Conrad had reached the final peak of his achievement and he wrote only one more novel: his swan-song, THE ROVER. The serene and idyllic tone of this narrative, which is nevertheless saturated with his familiar theme of conflict between society and its outcasts, makes manifest the peace of mind with which Conrad was at long last able to contemplate the phenomena that had troubled and harried him during his entire life. The obvious parallel, in the abstract, between the private life histories of Jean Peyrol and Joseph Conrad can mean only one thing: that Conrad meant THE ROVER to be an autobiographical pantomimic summing up of the essential features of his own career. Both Jean Peyrol and Joseph Conrad had in their old age brought glory on their native lands—lands which both had abandoned as young men under a cloud of blame. Conrad's success as a master in the field of English fiction made him one of the most distinguished Poles of his generation, and Jean Peyrol's success in carrying out the ruse which sent the British fleet scurrying away from French shores made him a national hero of Napoleonic France. And the similarity between the two is given an additional ironic twist by the fact that the honor and acclaim which both men deserve is extended to them first by the British and only afterwards by their own countrymen. After a lifetime of seeming non-conformity, each man had affirmed in his own way his feeling of identity with the society of his origin. They took the long way round to conformity, and their manner of expressing their conformity was not conventional, but they did arrive at last and did give expression to their feeling of emotional participation in the life of the large social group from which they sprang.

Just as THE BLACK MATE was a prefiguration of Conrad's entire subsequent work in fiction, so is THE ROVER in some degree a resumé of all the stories which preceded it and, in particular, a summary and final statement of the solved problem. The need of the non-conformist to find some way to give proof of the authenticity of his title to group membership: this is the burden of all Conrad's fiction. To win society's recognition of this fact about its non-conformists, while it may not have been an aim of which Conrad was wholly conscious, is nevertheless the inherent aim, the energizing principle, which exists at the very core of all the stories and novels that Conrad wrote. Were this recognition won, society would cease to feel the need to require of its non-conformists that they give up their non-conformity and by the same token the non-conformist himself would tend to take less neurotic attitudes to himself and to society.

The problem which absorbed all of Conrad's creative energies is today not only the personal problem of more individuals than in Conrad's time but also of a larger portion of the total number of human beings now living. With the growth in density of population, in rapidity of communication, and with industrialization, has come also, as a direct consequence thereof, a necessary systematic organizing of human beings into closely knit groups, industrial, social and economic. In the interest of sheer survival the individual human beings which make up mankind have been compelled by the pressure of circumstances to group themselves into multiform cooperative associations. This has happened not only in America but also all over the planet. Community life has become universal.

Human beings however are not by nature as social as ants or bees, and therefore the growth of community life has not gone unattended by outbreaks of exasperation on the part of numerous individuals who have found the conformities required of them to be unpalatable. On the other hand great numbers of people have been found to be remarkably amenable to the pressures of the prevailing conformities. It has therefore come about that among the pre- ·dominant characteristic phenomena of our time are mass flights into conformity, increases in the numbers of those made neurotic by suppression of non-conformist impulses, increases in the numbers of covert non-conformists, and a growing tendency among group leaders to take punitive action against overt non-conformists. Almost no one today escapes the task of taking a position with reference to group standards of one kind or another. Everyone must perforce find for himself one or another modus vivendi relative to the group or groups of which he is, often despite himself, a member. An underlying and often unconscious repugnance to, and chafing at, the pressures to conformity is perhaps one of the most universal feelings common to nearly all men and women of our time.

It is to this aspect of our contemporary psychological situation that Conrad speaks. What he has to say bears directly upon what is troubling us—not only in America but in all the rest of the world as well. As the earth's surface fills up with people social cohesion becomes more and more necessary, and individuals become more and more irked at the necessity. It was as if Conrad, so alive to the nature of his own predicament, had been a harbinger of things to come, because his work prophetically explains us to ourselves with more accuracy and understanding than that possessed by our contemporary writers. It is not my contention that Conrad BELIEVED anything, one way or the other, about society versus the individual; it is simply that he makes us more aware of all the implications of our own predicaments.

Many of us who read fiction quite probably realize but dimly just what it is in certain writers that draws us to them. We are prone to attribute the attraction to the incidental beauties, to the craftsmanship and power of language, manifest in the artistry of the writer. However, essential as these factors are in elicting from us a total response to the writer's work, the basic factor is quite certainly the bearing of the subject matter on issues which deeply trouble us. This, I think, has been specially true of Conrad and the readers who have been drawn to him in increasing numbers during the sixty years since he published his first novel. What troubled him and a few others sixty years ago now troubles nearly all of us. But we, when we look about us with dismay, can now recall that Conrad was here before us, and that, while here, he surveyed and mapped the spiritual country in which we now find ourselves. To read his forty-two novels and stories, guide-books to this land, is to have experiences which enable us to feel at home in our own world.

INDEX OF PRINCIPAL CHARACTERS.

212